The Paper Plate Escape

The Paper Plate Escape

The Prison Break that Broke the System

Dubs Byers

Dubs Byers
dubsbyers@protonmail.com

ISBN: 978-1-7337964-8-4

Photographs and diagrams: Dubs Byers
All photographs on pages 85–98 were taken in 1985.

Cover and book design: H. K. Stewart

Printed in the United States of America

This book is printed on archival-quality paper that meets requirements of the American National Standard for Information Sciences, Permanence of Paper, Printed Library Materials, ANSI Z39.48-1984.

To Jane Knight Byers,
my cheerleader, encourager, and life partner.
You are truly the wind beneath my wings.

Cummins Prison
Varner, Arkansas

(circa 1979)

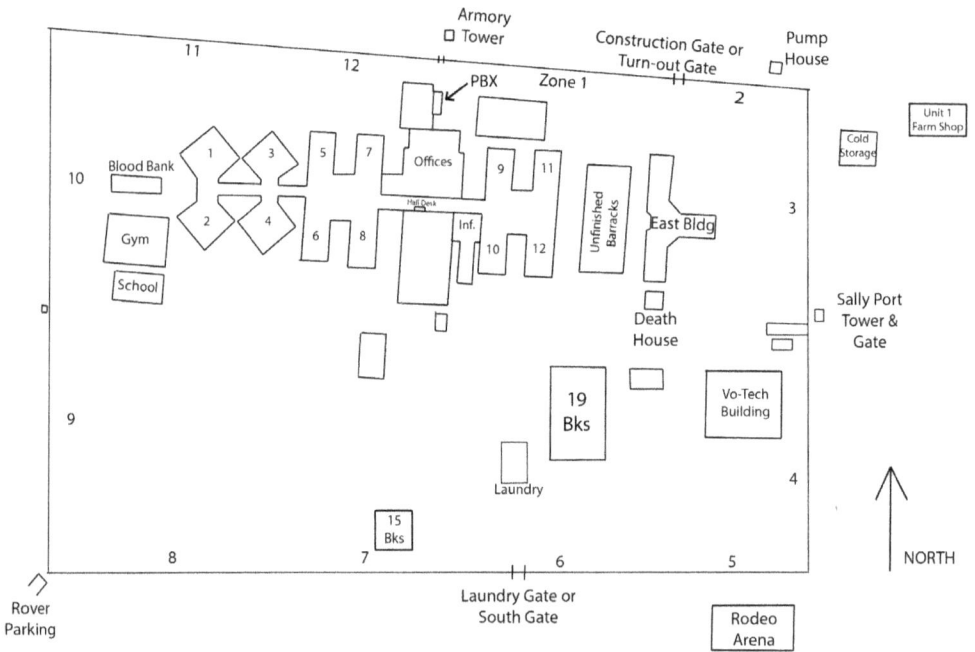

Farm Office

Armory
Tower

Construction Gate or
Turn-out Gate

Pump House

11

12

PBX

Zone 1

2

Cold Storage

Unit 1 Farm Shop

10

Blood Bank

1   3

5   7

Offices

9   11

3

2   4

6   8

Hall Desk

Inf.

10   12

Unfinished Barracks

East Bldg

Gym

School

Sally Port
Tower &
Gate

Death
House

9

19
Bks

Vo-Tech
Building

4

15
Bks

Laundry

8

7

6

5

NORTH

Rover
Parking

Laundry Gate or
South Gate

Rodeo
Arena

Contents

Acknowledgements

This work could not have been completed without the help of numerous people. Because this incident occurred in 1979, there are still many who are alive and have first-hand knowledge of that night. Much gratitude is due those who sat down and visited with me about the events of that night. I want to particularly thank Jane Byers, Judy Grimmett, Mary Jo Tucker, and George Brewer, who edited the work and provided pertinent advice for the improvement of the book. Thank you, one and all.

Introduction

Monday, January 1, 1979, was a pivotal day in the history of the Arkansas Department of Corrections (ADC). It started out like any other day inside a prison. It ended with a total take-over of the maximum security building that housed the worst of the worst inmates in Arkansas, including some on death row. Officers were assaulted and hostages were taken inside the building. Outside, 10 inmates scaled the fence and led officials on a 14-hour chase that ended in the capture of all escapees. But that's not the end of the story. What happened next would change the course of corrections in Arkansas for decades to come.

Chapter 1

A Brief History of Cummins

Cummins Prison has a long and notorious history. The story begins in 1902 when the state purchased the Cummins and Maple Grove plantations, a total of 10,000 acres, in the eastern part of Lincoln County adjacent to the Arkansas River. This was prime delta farmland, and the state was wanting to make a change in the way prisons were operated.

Before being moved to Lincoln County, the prison was in Little Rock, as it had been since 1842, when the first penitentiary was built on the land where the current state capitol stands. The prison was always expected to be self-sustaining, not costing the taxpayers anything to operate and maintain. To do this, the state eventually established the lease system, whereby inmates were leased out to private entities to provide labor for such things as farming, coal mining, and building trades. It did not take the state long to realize this was not a good idea. Inmates were beaten, worked long hours, and poorly fed. While the state recognized the abuses of the lease system, it did not have a viable alternative until the Cummins Farm was established in 1902, when the first inmates, along with some mules, were transferred to Cummins from Little Rock.

In moving to Cummins, the state slowly transitioned from the lease system, which was abolished in the 1910s, to a farming system, whereby inmate labor was used by the state to grow crops. The crops could provide sustenance for the inmates and animals, with the excess being sold to maintain and operate the prison. The prison was generally self-sufficient from its inception in 1842 to the late 1960s, when the trusty system was dismantled.

In the beginning, there were as many as seven "camps" scattered around the 10,000 acres that comprised the prison farm. Each camp had a large wooden structure that housed a number of inmates who were responsible for farming the area around their particular camp. In a 1915 report, seven camps were listed:

- **Lakeview Camp** (235 black male prisoners)
- **Goree Camp** (147 white male prisoners)
- **Middle Camp** (19 black female prisoners)
- **Back Camp** or **Woods Camp** (185 black male prisoners)
- **Willey Camp** (170 white male prisoners)
- **Front Camp** (361 black male prisoners)
- **Varner Camp** (53 black male prisoners)

This made a total of 1,170 inmates who were incarcerated at Cummins in 1915: 317 white males, 834 black males, and 19 black females.

The trusty system was developed so that inmates did almost all the work of running the prison. There was only a handful of freeworld employees, as few as six or seven at Cummins. These workers and their families lived on the prison grounds in houses on a road known as the "freeline." To supplement their meager state wages, they were furnished meat, milk, vegetables, and other supplies that were produced on the prison farm. These perks were known as emoluments. The few employees were expected to oversee more than a thousand inmates; thus inmates had to be enlisted to perform almost all the tasks, including guarding other inmates. As one might expect, if there were very little money expended for salaries, then the cost of running a prison could be kept to a bare minimum. There were many years that the prison turned a profit for the state.

Armed trusties were in charge of guarding the common inmates known as "rankers" or "rank-men." The trusties were armed with shotguns and rifles. They oversaw all the activities of the other prisoners, except for administering corporal punishment. This was reserved for the employees who were known as "whipping bosses." The whipping bosses used a long leather strap with a wooden handle on one end. The strap would be administered to the bare back and buttocks of the offending inmate. Corporal punishment was the only means of discipline and the fear of the strap was enough to keep most of the inmates in line. Years after the strap was discontinued, a former whipping boss who was a sergeant in the halls of Cummins was heard to say, "Man, I wish I had that strap back. The strap could make the lame to walk and the blind to see!"

The only problem was that the trusty system and the mode of discipline lent themselves to abuse. Trusties would use their position to extort money, sexual favors, and other resources from those whom they supervised. They could cause inmates to be whipped if they didn't like them or they didn't do as the trusty wanted. There is also evidence that the whippings went beyond discipline and bordered on sadomasochism. The federal court eventually found the trusty system as well as corporal punishment unconstitutional. In the late sixties and early seventies the ADC began to hire freeworld employees to do the jobs that were once done by the trusties. When corporal punishment was abolished, the only means of punishment was to place offenders in some form of punitive isolation (the "hole") and take away privileges other inmates had. One such example was the food they ate while in the hole. It was called gruel or grue, and it was a bland, baked cake containing all the kitchen leftovers from the day before.

In the 1940s, under the leadership of prison director Tom Cogbill and Governor Ben Laney, a new concept was born and the main building of present-day Cummins was built. The objective was to get all the inmates under one roof, thus making it easier to supervise and control them. The design was called telephone pole construction because the layout resembled a telephone pole with a long, wide hallway running east and west, and barracks built on either side and opening into the central hallway. When the initial construction was completed in the 1950s, there were four barracks on the West Hall and four barracks on the East Hall. Each barracks housed up to 100 men on bunks in neat rows with a commissary, a laundry picket, and a barber station, all of which were run by inmates. In addition, most of the security was provided by inmates. "Floor walkers" would be the equivalent of bar bouncers and were responsible for quelling any disturbance in the barracks. "Turn keys" were inmates assigned to open the iron bar doors of the barracks to let inmates come and go, and also to open the iron bar doors in the riot gates in the main hall.

After the Penitentiary Study Commission presented their report to the Arkansas Legislature in 1968, funds were appropriated by the legislature to build a new maximum security facility. The Maximum Security Unit, or East Building, was completed in 1971. It was a welcome replacement to the previous isolation facility at Cummins. The previous unit consisted of 12 cells, 11 of which were used to house inmates and one converted to a shower room. This isolation unit was at the center of a federal lawsuit, referred to as Holt v Sarver I, in 1969. Among other complaints, the inmates alleged that confinement in the isolation cells amounted to cruel and unusual punishment. Federal Judge J. Smith Henley ruled that being confined in an isolation cell at Cummins did, in fact, amount to cruel and unusual punishment. The cells were 10 feet by eight feet and generally housed four to 10 inmates. The plumbing was unsanitary and there was generally a strong stench in the cells. The mattresses were pulled out every day and there was no guarantee that an inmate would get the same mattress the next night, thus increasing the chance for the spreading of disease. The ruling read:

> The Court finds that the prolonged confinement of numbers of men in the same cell under the conditions that have been described is mentally and emotionally traumatic as well as physically uncomfortable. It is hazardous to health. It is degrading and debasing; it offends modern sensibilities, and, in the Court's estimation, amounts to cruel and unusual punishment. (Holt v. Sarver, 300 F. Supp. 825)

The construction of the East Building went a long way in alleviating the concerns the court had about those who were placed in isolation. It was a modern design with four-man cells, two-man cells, and single-man cells. It was a T-shaped building with wings running north, east, and south. It housed death row inmates, habitual trouble makers, escape risks, and inmates who were involved in killing other inmates, and provided punitive isolation for those guilty of disciplinary infractions and protective custody for those who for one reason or another needed to be protected from the general population,

By 1979, the total acreage had risen to over 16,000 acres and the inmate population had risen to 1,466. Along with the Maximum Security Building, four minimum security barracks had been built as an extension to the West Hall. These were 60-man, private cell barracks and most of them housed inmates who held some of the better jobs, like front office porters and clerks. All the occupants were class one inmates, which meant they had good institutional records and had been placed in a responsible job. A large metal building had been built in the southeast part of the compound. It was a large open barracks and housed approximately 60 inmates and was called Nineteen Barracks.

Chapter 2

A Day like Any Other

In the freeworld, New Year's Day is normally a time of watching parades and football on TV, visiting with friends, and perhaps enjoying some adult beverages during a state holiday which, in 1979, fell on a Monday, making for a three-day weekend. There were three bowl games on that day and many, both freeworld and inmates, gathered around the TVs to watch the action.

The freeworld people who lived on the grounds of Cummins Prison formed a tight-knit community. Housing and other amenities were provided for the upper level management of Cummins. The warden, assistant wardens, majors, captains, farm personnel, and even a few support personnel like chaplains and infirmary administrators lived on the "freeline" of Cummins along with their families. There were also other lower ranking security personnel who lived at "Eight Camp," a mobile home park located about two and a half miles from the unit, just west of Highway 65 at the junction of Highway 388, the turn off that goes to Cummins.

For most of the day, there was typical winter weather for Arkansas. The temperature started out in the low 30s with wind generally out of the north at 9–14 mph. While it remained in the upper 20s and lower 30s throughout the day, later that evening it would drop drastically, ending up in the low teens later in the night and throughout the next day with winds gusting 12-14 mph. The weather would play a major factor in how the events would transpire later in the evening.

The prison ran three shifts a day: 7:00 a.m.–3:00 p.m., 3:00 p.m.–11:00 p.m., and 11:00 p.m.–7:00 a.m. On the 3-11 shift that day 17 officers were on duty, with the highest-ranking officer being the shift lieutenant. Since it was a state holiday, many of the employees were off and only necessary employees, all officers, were present for the shift. Generally, there would be a building major on duty who was responsible for the security inside the building, but because of the holiday, the highest rank-ing officer at Cummins was the shift lieutenant. The shift lieu-tenant was the go-to supervisor in the building. He generally sat at the yard desk (also referred to as the hall desk) which was a large counter that sat in the middle of the hall where the hall from the front office area connected to the main hall along which the barracks were located. There might also be a sergeant or other officers there, but someone was always sitting at the yard desk. It was the nerve center for the whole building. No chow calls, infirmary calls, or program calls were given, and no inmates moved unless the yard desk was notified and cleared it. The yard desk controlled everything inside the fence, except for the East Building, which was the maximum security building.

The East Building was a closed organizational unit and had its own schedule and structure. On the 3-11 shift that night, there were 107 inmates assigned to the East Building and six officers on duty to supervise them. The officers included:

- **Sergeant L. O. Shugart** was the East Building supervisor that night. He was 39 years old and had worked at the ADC for 19 months. He had been a sergeant for about 11 months.

- **Officer Earnest Bryant** had been working at the ADC for three weeks when the incident occurred. He had worked in the East Building for four nights and under Sgt. Shugart for only two nights. He was 6'1" tall and weighed 170 pounds.

- **Officer Ronald Moon** had been working for the ADC for five weeks when the incident occurred. He was 19 years old.

- **Officer Michael Holmes** was 19 years old and had been working for the ADC for five months when the incident occurred.

- **Officer Ralph Perry** was 19 years old and had been working at the ADC for two weeks. He had been working in the East Building for a night and a half when the incident occurred.

- **Officer Elvis Brown** had been employed by the ADC for a little over six months when the incident occurred.

What strikes the casual observer is the youthfulness and lack of experience of the officers who were on duty that night. They were expected to supervise and control the most hardened prisoners in the state of Arkansas. Not only were the inmates more skilled in personal use of force, but they were also more adept in manipulating others for their own nefarious purposes.

Chapter 3

The Setup

The development of the circumstances that eventually led to the takeover of the East Building and the escape of multiple inmates didn't just happen. It was not a spontaneous event. It was carefully and thoughtfully planned. There were two inmates who were key players; one was the mastermind and the other was the muscle.

Inmate Barney Norton was the mastermind. Norton was a 41-year-old white male and had been in the ADC since September 8, 1975. He was convicted of assault with intent to kill in Garland County, Arkansas, and was given a 30-year sentence. Upon intake into the ADC, he had very little to say. He stated what he was accused of but said he was not guilty of the charge. He also stated that he had no prior convictions. He listed his mother, Jessie Norton, as a minister from Amity, Arkansas.

Norton, along with a death row inmate, Earl Van Denton, had a previous escape just a few months earlier, on September 17, 1978. Both inmates were assigned to the East Building at the time, and it was reported that they used art supplies to dye their white uniforms to a dark color. They somehow were able to pick the locks to their cell doors and make their way out an end door of the building. As they climbed the fence, an officer in a nearby tower yelled at them to halt but did not fire his weapon. Norton was captured an hour and a half later less than a mile from the prison. Van Denton fared better. He remained at large for about five hours before dogs tracked him down near the small town of Gould.

It is safe to say that Inmate Norton was 100 percent for himself and other inmates and 100 percent against the officers and administration. In a conversation with A. L. "Art" Lockhart not long after Lockhart became warden at Cummins, Norton let Lockhart know that he (Norton) knew which house Lockhart lived in, what time his wife left for her job at the local school, where she parked her car at the school, and how many children Lockhart had. He did this in an attempt to scare Lockhart into reversing a decision that was detrimental to Norton. Inmate Norton's strategy did not work with Lockhart. After the discussion, Lockhart told Norton that he was going to go home, take a sip of whiskey, and forget the conversation that he had with Norton.

From all accounts Norton was rebellious toward the rules of the institution and uncooperative with any questioning that might explain his behavior or the behavior of his fellow inmates. When questioned, he always maintained his innocence and his non-involvement in any situation. Because of his consistently rebellious attitude, he was highly respected among the inmate population and equally disliked by his free world supervisors and administration. One inmate, who was not involved in the incident that night, described him as the Don (Mafia boss) of the inmate population. He indicated that Norton was well-respected among inmates and was into selling drugs and bootleg. He was the go-to guy if an inmate needed something. Norton dealt in favors and contraband.

It was Inmate Norton who helped Inmate Johnny Wiggins in his ability to develop trust among his supervisors. One witness indicated that Inmate Norton may have helped Inmate Wiggins by providing him with money so that he could buy soft drinks and treats for the officers. If this report is true, then it was Norton who helped groom Wiggins into a "somewhat trusted convict," as Wiggins was described in one of the investigation reports. Wiggins needed that status to be able to tip over the first domino in a long chain of events that night. He was a porter in the East Building. A porter is responsible for cleaning and mopping the area to which he is assigned, so he generally had access to most of the East Building.

Inmate Wiggins was a 27-year-old white male and had been in the ADC since January 27, 1978. It should also be noted that he was 6'2" and weighed 178 pounds, which made him taller and heavier than most inmates at the time. He was doing a 20-year sentence for Aggravated Robbery and Theft of Property out of Washington County, Arkansas. He admitted upon intake that he had escaped from McAlester Prison in Oklahoma, where he was serving time for First Degree Manslaughter. After escaping from McAlester, he and his accomplice then came to Arkansas, kidnapped a woman in Springdale, robbed her and took her car, thus picking up the charge for which he was currently serving time in Arkansas.

How does one become "a somewhat trusted convict?" It takes time and effort. It takes time, in that trust is not earned quickly, but must be garnered over a span of time with a series of small events that develop trust. It takes effort, in that the person must consistently conform to prison rules and do the job assigned to him in an exemplary fashion so that he can accumulate favor from his supervisors. It also helps if one is proficient in using manipulative skills. Many inmates are accomplished in this area. They know how to build trust and confidence so that they can later use these to execute an escape.

Chapter 4

The Takeover

A night or two before the takeover, Norton had gotten word
to certain key inmates who were assigned to the East Building
to be in either one of the two dayrooms on the night of
January 1. The dayrooms were in the central part of the building just behind the Control Room. The dayrooms themselves
could be visually monitored by the Control Room, but the doors
leading into the dayrooms were accessed from the wings and
the activity outside the dayroom doors could not be easily monitored by the Control Room officer. The dayrooms were multi-
purpose spaces that were used for such things as programming,
religious services, and "recreation call." Recreation call was
basically a time for approved inmates to get out of their cells
and congregate and watch TV. The call was given each weekday
night 7:00 p.m.–10:30 p.m.

That night, there were 12 inmates in each of the dayrooms.
The Orange Bowl was on the TVs in the dayrooms. Fourth-ranked
Oklahoma was playing Big Eight rival, sixth-ranked Nebraska.
The game started at 7:00 p.m., but by the time it was over, none
of the inmates would know that Oklahoma had bested Nebraska
31-24 and earned a shot at the national championship. There was

a much more spellbinding game being played out in the East Building by 10:00 p.m.

While the names of all the inmates in the dayrooms are unknown, the witness statements indicate that Inmates Barney Norton, Glenn Blaylock, Gary Morse, and Ronnie Pucilowski were in Dayroom 1, while Inmates Jerome Bargo and Ismet Divanovich were in Dayroom 2. There were others in the dayrooms who did not participate in the events of that night. As events unfolded and inmates took over the East Building, there were those who remained in the dayrooms and caused no trouble until the East Building was finally taken back over by freeworld personnel.

Things were hectic that night. There were a lot of moving parts. There is no way to determine precisely what happened and the proper sequence of events. However, upon examining all the officer and inmate witness statements from that night, the following narrative seems to be a logical series of events.

As stated earlier, Inmate Barney Norton had gotten word out a day or two earlier for certain inmates to be in the dayrooms the night of January 1. It appears that Norton had hatched a plan for certain inmates to escape. The inmates had been allowed to come to the dayroom at approximately 6:00 p.m. They had been in the dayrooms for more than two hours. Since there was no bathroom in the dayrooms, officers would give a bathroom break every hour to hour and a half. Inmates needing to go to the bathroom would be escorted out of the dayroom and across the hall to a bathroom. The inmates had already been given one bathroom break around 7:30-8:00 p.m. At approximately 9:00 p.m., Inmate Johnny Wiggins, the East Building porter, knocked on the Dayroom 1 door and was allowed to come out. He made his way to the Control Room area. Very soon after this, Inmate Ronnie Pucilowski knocked on the dayroom door and said that he "needed to go to the bathroom bad." Officer Moon told Inmate Pucilowski that he had already had his "piss call," which is what the inmates and officers called the bathroom break. Officer Holmes then told Pucilowski that he would let him go this time, and Officer Holmes yelled for Officer Bryant, who was in the Control Room, to electronically open Dayroom 1 door. The door to the dayroom popped open.

There were four officers (Brown, Moon, Perry, and Holmes) just outside Dayroom 1. When the door opened, Inmates Norton, Blaylock, Morse, and Pucilowski rushed the officers and pushed them against the wall, overpowering them and taking at least one baton and a slapper. A slapper is a small, leather hand-held weapon approximately one foot in length with a grip on one end and a round piece of lead sewn into the leather head of the weapon which made for a heavy hit when swung on someone. The slapper was a favorite weapon of officers during this era. The inmates then pushed Officers Brown, Perry, and Holmes back into the dayroom and slammed the door shut, thus locking them inside. Officer Moon was outside the dayroom in the hallway. After Officer Bryant had popped the Dayroom 1 door, but before he knew there was any kind of disturbance, Inmate Wiggins knocked on the door of the Control Room and told Officer Bryant that Sgt. Shugart needed a paper plate.

Officer Bryant had no intention of letting Inmate Wiggins into the Control Room. He knew that there were no inmates allowed in there, but here was a porter, a "somewhat trusted inmate," knocking on his door and telling him that the supervisor of the East Building needed a plate from the Control Room. Officer Bryant got the paper plate and opened the door and was going to hand the plate to Inmate Wiggins. When the door opened, Inmate Wiggins forced himself into the Control Room, pushed Officer Bryant back, then grabbed a baton that was on the closed-circuit TV and hit Officer Bryant with all the force he could muster causing a large gash on the officer's head and driving him to the floor. Inmate Wiggins then obtained a set of handcuffs and handcuffed Officer Bryant's hands behind his back.

Chapter 5

The Chaos

With the officers overpowered and Inmate Wiggins in the Control Room, all hell broke loose. As Sgt. Shugart later said in his witness statement, everything was like a "darn Keystone Cop movie." And it was. The events that followed are sketchy. They may not be rendered in exactly the sequence in which they occurred, but all the following events happened during the 20 to 30 minutes that the inmates were in control of the building.

It should be noted that there was very little resistance on the part of the officers during the takeover. Perhaps they realized early on that they were outmanned and defenseless or perhaps their youthfulness and lack of adequate training prevented them from knowing what to do when faced with a circumstance such as this. They may have been by nature generally passive and non-aggressive. Their passivity was expressed at one point during the takeover while they were being held hostage. Officer Brown and Sgt. Shugart both admitted to Inmate Earl Van Denton, who was guarding them, that they were not violent people. The only semblance of resistance was when Inmate Norton demanded that Sgt. Shugart come out of his uniform. He ignored the demand and kept his uniform on. Nothing else was said about the matter.

Officers Brown, Moon, Perry, and Holmes were ordered to lie face down in the hallway. Three of them, Brown, Moon, and Holmes, were ordered to come out of their uniforms, which they did. The four were then escorted to Cell #12 on the South Wing and locked inside.

Meanwhile, in the Control Room, Inmates Wiggins and Norton were grabbing keys and going to cells throughout the East Building and unlocking them. There were a few doors, like the front door and the doors leading into the various pods, that were electronically controlled, but all the inmate cells had to be opened with a key. As Norton and others made the rounds and opened cell doors, some inmates came out; many did not. Of the 107 inmates assigned to the East Building that night, only 18 would come out of their assigned area and participate in the insurrection. Many just locked their cell doors back and waited out the siege.

During the melee, Sgt. Shugart was determined to get to the Control Room to check on Officer Bryant. As Shugart finally reached the Control Room, he was handcuffed and held hostage. Both Sgt. Shugart and Officer Bryant were later taken to Cell #12 and locked in with the other four officers. Officer Bryant was apparently escorted to Cell #12 by Inmate Jerome Bargo and another inmate. Inmate Bargo said that he got a towel and placed it against Bryant's head in an effort to try to suppress the bleeding. He also said that Bryant was capable enough to walk to Cell #12 under his own strength.

The inmates who were planning to escape were told to go to the clothing room and get the clothing they needed for the weather conditions outside. Along with inmate field jackets, inmates snatched up state issued long underwear, socks, and sock caps. Some of them also had various pieces of officer uniforms that had been confiscated, along with an officer coat or two. Even though the inmates may have thought they had adequate clothing for their escape attempt, it became obvious that they were woefully unprepared for the eight-degree weather and howling winds they were about to encounter.

After obtaining clothes, a few supplies, and a small amount of snack food, the inmates met in the lobby area in front of the Control Room and made their way out of the East Building and toward different areas of the perimeter fence. Seven inmates headed north toward the fence and three headed south to the fence behind the laundry. At that time, there was only one 10-foot chain link fence surrounding Cummins with some strands of barbed wire along the top. For a skilled person and with the aid of a sheet or similar object to throw over the barbed wire at the top, it was not too difficult to scale the fence, and this is what the inmates did. But more about them later.

Back in the East Building, there were at least five more inmates, four of whom were on death row, who were planning to escape, but they were a few seconds behind the first wave. These five (Inmates Paul Ruiz, Earl Van Denton, Charles Pickens, Charles Neal, and Calvin Ford) made their way out of the East Building and started walking to the end of the building toward the Death House, which is located on the south end of the East Building. About the time they got to the Death House area, the officer in the Sally Port Tower and the officer in the main Armory Tower started shooting at the inmates who were scaling the fence. In the Sally Port Tower, 18-year-old Officer Melvin Wiley fired one warning shot with his AR-15 when he saw the first inmate going over the fence near Zone 2, which is on the north side of the compound. He fired six more shots at four inmates as they scaled the fence and started running east away from the compound. No one was hit. The officer in the Armory Tower, located at the front of the compound, which is on the north side, about midway in the fence that runs east and west, had an M-1 Carbine Rifle. He fired one warning shot and four additional shots at the fleeing inmates. He did not hit any of the inmates, but he did manage to clip an electric line that fed electricity to the front entrance area. With no electricity the officer was unable to open the front gate electronically, so employees needing to enter the main building had to climb the chain-link gate and manually release the mechanism that opened the gate.

The shots frightened the five inmates near the Death House because they could not tell from which direction the officers were shooting, and they thought they were the targets of the bullets. Four of the inmates returned to the East Building. Inmate Calvin Ford headed west and walked the entire length of the compound, came to the exterior door at the west end of the hall, and turned on the light which signaled to officers on the inside of the building that there was someone outside who was wanting to enter the building. Lt. Gaylon Lay had just arrived at the unit and as he walked back to the hall desk, he noticed the light on the West Hall door blinking on and off. He got the key, opened the door, and saw Inmate Ford, whom he recognized as an inmate, standing outside the door in an officer's uniform and jacket, holding a riot baton. He ordered Ford to give him the baton, which he did. He then handcuffed Ford and escorted him to the Hall Desk, where he stood for some length of time.

Paul Ruiz was frightened and agitated by the shooting. He was relatively sure that the shooting was aimed at him and his cohorts. When he returned to the East Building, he became the principal leader after the others had escaped and before the liberation by the officers.

If there was one inmate who took control inside the East Building after Norton and the others had escaped, it was Paul Ruiz. He, along with his fall partner, Earl Van Denton was on death row for killing Magazine Town Marshall Marvin Richie and Park Ranger Opal James in 1977 after they had escaped from a work detail at the Oklahoma State Prison in McAlester, Oklahoma. It is believed that after their escape from Oklahoma, they left a trail of murder of at least four people in Oklahoma and Louisiana before ending up in Logan County, Arkansas, where two more were killed and another seriously injured. Paul Ruiz was a cold-blooded killer and would eventually be executed for his crimes in 1997.

During the cold night of January 1, however, Ruiz became the commandant of the East Building. He issued the orders. He demanded that two officers (Brown and Holmes) be brought to the Control Room to make phone calls to the officers in the tower and main building. He made death threats if his demands were not met. He told the employees to get away from the front door or the officers inside would be hurt or killed. He made threatening gestures toward the officer in the Control Room as the employees on the outside were attempting to gain access to the East Building. He was so out of control that even his own fall partner, Van Denton, handed the cell keys back to Sgt. Schubert and asked Schubert to lock him back in his cell because he no longer wanted to be a part of what was going on. It was reported by the officers that there was an ongoing argument between Ruiz and Van Denton. Ruiz wanted to "kill him a pig," but Van Denton kept telling him there was no use in that. Ruiz eventually came down to Van Denton's cell and seeing Van Denton back in his cell, commented to Van Denton, "You're gonna keep your damn ass in there and I'm gonna leave." Ruiz then went back up front.

During all the chaos of the "Keystone Cops" saga, there was an action taken by one of the officers that probably saved lives. Early on, when all the keys were being taken out of the Control Room by Inmate Norton and others, Officer Brown was able to knock two cell keys into a trash can where they would not be discovered. Whether Officer Brown knew whose cells those keys belonged to is unknown, but one of the keys opened the cell of Inmate John Swindler. If Swindler had been able to get out of his cell, the events of that night probably would have been far different … and far worse.

Inmate John Edward Swindler was on death row for killing Fort Smith Patrolman Randy Basnett in 1976. Swindler, who was illiterate, had stopped at a service station to ask for directions to Kansas. He had previously been incarcerated at Leavenworth in Kansas and was allegedly on his way back to Kansas to settle some old scores from when he was in prison there. He was spotted and questioned by Patrolman Basnet at the service station. Swindler, while sitting in the driver's seat of a stolen vehicle, raised a .25 caliber pistol and shot Basnet twice in the chest. Basnet died while being transported to the hospital.

After Swindler was released from Leavenworth in Kansas, and before he came to Arkansas, he abducted Dorothy Ann Rhodes, 18, and Greg Becknell, 19, in Columbia, South Carolina. Rhodes and Becknell were girlfriend and boyfriend. While he was on death row in Arkansas, he boasted about his crime, stating that the girl (Dorothy Rhodes) was surprised when Swindler "went down on" (sexually assaulted) her boyfriend, Greg Becknell, instead of sexually assaulting her. Swindler later killed both, shooting them in the head. He was also charged but never convicted of killing a Pennsylvania student in Florida.

These crimes, along with his behavior on death row, substantiated the idea that Swindler was a cold-blooded killer with little or no conscience. He made it evident during his incarceration that he had regard for no one and had no value for human life, especially African Americans. G. B. Davis, a black teacher at the Cummins Unit School at that time, was tasked with going to the

East Building several times a week to provide educational material and one-on-one instruction for those assigned to the East Building. Davis related that on more than one occasion, as he passed by Swindler's cell, Swindler would shout out, "Mr. Davis, when I get out of here, I'm going to kill all the n*****s and you're going to be the first one I kill." On the night of January 1, there were six officers on duty in the East Building. Five were African American. Swindler desperately wanted out of his cell to join the fracas. He banged on the door and was heard yelling for someone to let him out. One can see the complications that might have come about if Swindler had been let out of his cell. Events could have been far worse if not for the actions of Officer Brown.

Even in death, Swindler expressed his rebellion to authority. When he was convicted in 1976, the electric chair was the mode of carrying out the death penalty. That changed in 1983 when lethal injection was passed into law. Since Swindler was sentenced to die in the electric chair in 1976 and in the seven-year interim the method of execution had changed to lethal injection, Swindler was given the choice of either the chair or lethal injection. He refused to make a choice. Because he failed to choose, he was executed in the electric chair on June 19, 1990, as he was originally sentenced. He was the last person to die in the electric chair in Arkansas. One official in the Department of Corrections expressed the belief that Swindler, by not choosing, chose the electric chair because he did not want to look weak by opting for the less painful form of execution.

As prison officials were being notified about a disturbance, they at first thought they were just dealing with an escape. The officials being called by the PBX operator were told that there were approximately six inmates who had gone over the fence. In 1979, the phone calls going in and out of the prison unit were controlled by the PBX operator. PBX is an abbreviation for "private branch exchange," which is another term for a private telephone switchboard. The PBX operator was located near the front entrance of the building in a small, self-contained room with glass on all sides. Imagine the old photographs of telephone operators who were seated at a large control panel, constantly inserting plugs to connect calls. That, on a smaller scale, was the PBX. The PBX operator had to connect any call going into or out of the prison. The PBX operator, then, was an important link in an emergency. Many times, the operator was the person who contacted key prison personnel during a crisis. When the operator was getting out the word, she was unaware of the takeover in the East Building. All she knew was that there was an escape involving several inmates. It was not until Major B. G. Taylor had made his way into the main building that he learned that inmates had taken over the East Building. He then got word to Warden Jerry Campbell who in turn told Assistant Director Lockhart. Both men were in their vehicles on the levee which was near the freeline. They were making sure that the inmates were not heading to the freeline where many of the families of officials lived.

Chapter 6

Taking Back the East Building

When Mr. Lockhart heard about the hostage situation, he directed employees to gather at the Sally Port Gate, which is near the East Building. There were nine to 12 individuals who armed themselves with rifles, shotguns, and pistols and proceeded through the Sally Port Gate to the front door of the East Building, a distance of about 600 feet. The persons identified in the witness reports as being at the front door included Asst. Director A. L. Lockhart, Warden Jerry Campbell, Assistant Warden Larry Norris, Field Major Dale Reed, Captain Johnny King, Robert Rhoden, Ross Wayne Martin, Phillip Higginbotham, Building Major Billy Taylor, and State Police Criminal Investigation Division (CID) Investigator Jack Ursery. Mr. Lockhart had a shotgun, but while he was at Sally Port before he went in, he took all the pellets out of the shell that would be chambered when they entered the East Building. He did this for two reasons. First, he knew that he would be the first one to enter the East Building, and he didn't want to take the chance of having the weapon taken away from him with a live round inside. Second, if he needed to fire a round, the empty shell would just make a loud noise and would hopefully cause a distraction and not hit anyone. He also said that he asked Jack Ursery to have a live round in his shotgun and to follow Lockhart in and be a backup in case deadly force was needed.

When they arrived at the front door of the East Building, they found that it was locked. The door was controlled electronically from the Control Room and Inmate Ruiz refused to open the door. Assistant Warden Larry Norris was dispatched to the Armory Tower at the front of the prison, where he was to meet Assistant Warden Steve Bertschy who was retrieving an East Building front door key from the vault in the assistant warden's office. There were two inmates, Paul Ruiz and Willie Brown, and two officers, Elvis Brown and Michael Holmes, in the Control Room. It was hard to tell who was who, however, because one of the inmates had on an officer's uniform and at least one of the officers had on an inmate's uniform.

Mr. Lockhart was the main spokesperson and yelled for Ruiz to open the door. Ruiz refused. Ruiz told the two officers who were in the Control Room that they were going to die if they didn't get the employees away from the front door. Ruiz sent Officer Holmes out of the Control Room to the front door to convey that message to Mr. Lockhart. Mr. Lockhart told Officer Holmes to open the front door and the employees would handle it, but Officer Holmes refused, stating that if he opened the door then officers would be killed. He was convinced that Ruiz meant business. Inmate Ruiz was witnessed several times slamming one of the officers in the Control Room against the window and drawing back the baton in a threatening fashion as if he were going to strike the officer. Ruiz was advised by Lockhart that there was no way out, that no one would be permitted to leave with or without a hostage, and that the employees were not going to back away from the front door. Captain Kenny Taylor, who was obviously under the influence of alcohol that was consumed throughout the day, begged Lockhart to allow him to shoot his high-powered rifle at the plexiglass window beside the front door. No one knew what would happen if plexiglass was shot at close range by a rifle, and Lockhart did not allow him to find out.

Officer Brown was then sent to the front door to tell the employees to back off. Mr. Lockhart told Officer Brown just to sit down by the front door and he would be safe. Officer Brown did as he was directed. The employees then noticed that the key to the Control Room was left in one of the Control Room doors, and Officer Brown was told to get the key and slide it under the front door to Mr. Lockhart. Officer Brown did as he was instructed, and when Mr. Lockhart held the key up so that Ruiz could see what was in his hand, Ruiz popped the front door open and lay face down in the Control Room with his hands behind his back. At that point, Ruiz knew that it was over. Inmate Willie Brown, who was also in the Control Room, left the front area and ran down South Wing. His intention was to get back in his cell as the officers came in. His cell door, however, was locked and he could not get in, so he headed to the end of the South Wing where the quiet cells were located. Quiet cells were cells in which inmates who needed constant supervision were locked. There was an area outside the quiet cell where an officer could sit and constantly supervise the inmate in the cell. Inmate Brown hid in this small area.

Mr. Lockhart and the other employees entered the East Building and secured the Control Room first, placing Inmate Ruiz in handcuffs, stripping him of the officer's uniform, and leading him out of the Control Room to the lobby area. He was held in the lobby area for several hours, guarded primarily by Captain A. G. Lucas, the food service supervisor, and Lt. E. W. Smith. After the Control Room was secure, the officers started a methodical search of the East Building and began locking inmates back in their cells. Reports indicate that officers were met with no resistance. It was also noted that officers were armed with riot sticks, shotguns, and rifles, which may explain why there was no resistance. Most inmates never came out of their cells during the incident, so it was just a matter of making sure that inmates were in their proper cells and the cell doors were securely locked. There were also inmates in the dayrooms who had to be returned to their cells.

When officers searched the North Wing, they found the four officers in Cell #12. They included Sgt. Shugart and Officers Bryant, Moon, and Perry. Inmates Charles Neal and Charles Pickens were also in the cell with the officers. Both inmates were death row inmates and Cell #12 was their cell. Officer Bryant was partially handcuffed. Apparently one of the cuffs had been loosed, but the other remained on his wrist. There was also a set of handcuffs hanging on the inside doorknob of the cell. These were previously on Sgt. Shugart but had been picked off earlier in the cell using a plastic spoon. Sgt. Shugart had then hung them on the doorknob thinking they might be used to pull on and hold the door closed if any inmates came to get them. Once the officers were freed from the cell, Officer Bryant was taken to the infirmary where he received 19 stitches to the wound on his head.

During the takeover, a strange connection formed between the officers being held hostage in Cell #12 and the normal occupants of that cell, Death Row Inmates Neal and Pickens. Both these inmates had earlier left the East Building in hopes of escape but returned when shots were fired from the tower officers. They made their way back down the hall and for a moment stood outside their cell, now occupied by four officers. They finally opened the door and came in and took off their coats and sat down in the cell. One of them, probably Inmate Neal, got a towel and wet it with cold water and tried to stop the bleeding on the head of

Officer Bryant. Inmate Neal had a paper clip and attempted to pick the lock off the cuffs of Officer Bryant. He apparently partially succeeded because when the officers were liberated, Officer Bryant had one hand uncuffed.

Once the building was secure, Mr. Lockhart told Major B. G. Taylor to run a cell check and determine who was missing from the East Building. Major Taylor enlisted the help of Kenny Taylor, East Building Captain. The following inmates were missing from their cells: Inmates Barney Norton, Jerome Bargo, Gary Morse, Ronnie Pucilowski, Johnny Wiggins, Glen Blaylock, Ismet Divanovich, Ronnie Briggs, Terry Howell, Jerry McKee and Calvin Ford. Major Taylor stated that Ford was standing in front of the Hall Desk in the main building, so that left 10 inmates unaccounted for who had either escaped or were hiding somewhere inside the compound. As officials would soon learn, all 10 maximum security inmates made it over the fence and were on a run for their lives.

Chapter 7

The Escapes

The weather played a significant factor in the events of the night of January 1 and morning of January 2. The weather is the first thing mentioned by anyone who was involved in the events of that night. Many acknowledge that it was the coldest they had ever been. The temperature would eventually drop to eight degrees, with the winds gusting 12-15 mph. The chill factor hovered around 20 below zero. Earlier in the day on January 1, however, had not been all that bad. It was a typical winter day. There had been some scattered light freezing rain and sleet, but that was over by 8:00 a.m. Throughout the day on January 1, the temperature was in the mid to upper 20s with an overcast sky. However, the winds were consistently out of the north. By the time the inmates took over the building at 9:45 p.m., the sky was clearing, the temperature had dropped to the mid-teens, and the wind was gusting out of the north and northwest at 12 to 14 miles per hour. It was not a good evening to make one's way through mud, sloughs, and drainage ditches with clothing and footwear that were totally inadequate for the conditions.

The officials were sure that several inmates had scaled the fence and escaped, but they did not know how many. Neither did they know that all the inmates who left the East Building had, in fact, gone over the fence. There was a chance that some were hiding inside the compound, so no fewer than 10 officers were tasked with shaking down a dozen or so buildings inside the fence. This was done simultaneously while other officers geared up and began the search for the escapees on the outside of the compound. It was soon determined that all 10 missing inmates had gone over the fence and were on the run.

The chain link fence around the compound was 10 feet tall. At the top was a barbed-wire arm at a 45-degree angle leaning toward the inside of the fence. It had three strands of barbed wire running parallel to the fence, thus making it more difficult to climb over the fence. The Construction Gate and Laundry Gate would have been easier to scale, however, because they only had some strands of barbed wire that ran on the same plane as the fence, which made it a little easier to climb over.

The chain link fence with the slanted arm on top was a vast improvement over the security system of earlier times. In the early history of Cummins, trusties with high-powered rifles were placed at opposite corners of the arbitrary perimeter and ordered to shoot any inmate who wandered too close to the two perpendicular perimeters they were guarding. It was the equivalent of drawing a line in the sand and telling the inmates not to get near the line and for certain, not cross it lest they be shot. Apparently, it was not an unusual occurrence for inmates to be shot, and sometimes killed, as they wandered too close or past the line.

By 1979, progress had been made in securing the perimeter of the prison, even if the desire of the inmates to escape had not changed. In addition to the fence, there was a security system near the fence that detected movement when someone or something got close to the perimeter. This system was developed by

Westinghouse during the Viet Nam War period and was called a paraguard system. There was flexible tubing buried in sandy loam approximately one foot underneath the ground. The tubing had a semi-liquid gel in it and when any weight pressed down on the ground above it, the fluid moved and set off an alarm on a control panel in the armory tower. The officer could look at the panel, identify the zone where there might be trouble, and dispatch security personnel to check out that area of the fence. The problem with the paraguard system was that it was in constant need of repair, and it frequently set off false alarms.

The perimeter fencing was a large rectangle approximately 1,600 feet by 1,000 feet. The long sides ran east and west, while the short sides ran north and south. The perimeter was divided into 12 zones. Zone One started at the base of the Armory Tower and subsequent zones continued in a clockwise direction around the compound, with each zone covering approximately 500 feet of the periphery.

There were two main entrances into Cummins. The Armory Tower was located on the north side, about in the middle of the perimeter. All the foot traffic went through the gate by the Armory Tower. The base of the tower was used to store the weapons, ammunition, and other security devices that were used by security personnel. The officer in the tower electronically controlled the front gate as well as monitored the security of the perimeter, both visually and with the help of the paraguard system. There were large spotlights located on top of all the towers which allowed the officer to light up any part of the compound that needed checking. From time to time, the Armory Tower officer would institute a "light check," which meant he would shine a light on another tower and the officer in that tower was to shine his light back, thus making sure that the officer was alert and awake.

The Sally Port Tower and Gate were located about midway on the eastern perimeter. All vehicle traffic entered the compound through this gate. A vehicle would drive into an enclosed area, be searched, and then allowed access into the compound. The tower was located beside the gate, just outside the fence. The officer in the tower oversaw the traffic going into and out of the compound, as well as constantly guarding the perimeter.

Because the two main towers were located on the north and east sides of the perimeter, the west and south sides were more vulnerable. To compensate for this, an officer, called a rover, was stationed in a vehicle at the southwest corner of the perimeter. He was responsible for watching the west and south sides, as well as responding to any area of the fence when contacted by radio from the Armory Tower. Typically, the Armory Tower officer would radio the rover and tell him to check out a certain zone along the fence. The rover would then go to that zone, make a visual inspection of the area, and report back to the officer in the Armory Tower. The rover was also responsible for watching for any vehicle traffic that might approach the compound from the many small roads and turn rows that were in the fields around Cummins.

On the night of January 1, shortly before 10:00 p.m., Sally Port Gate Officer Melvin Wiley stood up to wipe the windows in the tower that were constantly fogging up and freezing. As he looked out, he saw what looked like a sheet (it was probably a laundry bag) draped over the fence in Zone Two on the north side of the compound. He then observed an inmate going over the fence. He fired a warning shot with his AR-15. He then observed four more attempting to scale the fence. When the warning shot was fired, two of the inmates turned back, but two continued to climb the fence. He fired six more shots at the escapees but failed to hit anyone. The Armory Tower officer also fired a warning shot with his M-1 rifle plus four more shots at the inmates but missed.

Inmate John Thornburg was manning the pump house just outside the fence near the northeast corner. The pump house had an inmate worker who monitored it 24 hours a day because if there were a problem, sewer would quickly back up into the building. Inmate Thornburg stated that when he heard a commotion, he saw four inmates standing outside the fence near the old turnout gate while a fifth was making his way over the fence. Inmate Thornburg stated that he then got inside the pumphouse and secured the door so they "could not get in on me." The inmates ran past the pumphouse and proceeded in a due east direction away from the compound. In all, seven inmates went over the fence at Zone 2. All of them ran due east, but they did not all stay together once they got away from the compound.

At this same time, three other inmates were seeking a place to scale the fence on the south side. Officer Robert Toney, who was in the rover vehicle at the southwest corner, thought he saw something run across the road that parallels the fence near the southeast corner close to the rodeo arena. When he made his way to Zone 5 and 6, he found only two dogs in the area. He returned to his parking place some 1,600 feet to the west. A minute or two later he was advised by the Armory Tower officer to check Zone 5. When he arrived, he found Inmate Ismet Divanovich, a native of Yugoslavia, struggling to get over the fence. Divanovich was not a U.S. citizen, had a very heavy accent, and was doing a life sentence for capital murder for killing an elderly woman in Garland County. He was told about the possible escape attempt by Inmate Jerome Bargo, his cell mate, the night before the incident and the two of them were waiting in Dayroom 2 for the disturbance to go down.

When Officer Toney approached Zone 5, he attempted to fire a warning shot, but said his AR-15 jammed. At about this same time, however, Assistant Warden Larry Norris and Field Major Dale Reed were approaching the scene from the opposite direction. Upon seeing Inmate Divanovich on the fence, Norris, who was driving, told Reed to "shoot the son of a bitch." Reed was holding a shotgun and had to get the long gun out of the window on the passenger's side and then hang the upper part of his body out of the window to fire the weapon. Just about the time Reed was ready to shoot, the car hit a mud puddle and ice-cold water sprayed up in Reed's face thus temporarily blinding him and likely saving Divanovich's life. When Divanovich reached the ground, he was apprehended. While Norris covered the rover's position, Reed and Toney took Divanovich to the front gate in the rover vehicle and he was turned over to Building Major Billy Taylor. The official CID report indicates that Major Taylor took Divanovich to the Building Major's office and began interrogating him. Divanovich told Taylor that there were approximately 15 inmates who escaped and one officer was badly injured inside the East Building. The major was later joined by Lt. Gaylon Lay and the interrogation continued. As Major Taylor was eventually needed at the East Building, he turned Divanovich over to Sgt. Smith (first name not listed) and told him to take Divanovich to the infirmary to be checked out and then return him to the East Building. One down, nine to go.

In an amended witness statement a week after the incident, Officer R. C. Toney, the rover officer, stated that he saw *two* inmates going over the fence. The inmate in the lead got over the fence and fled in the darkness. The second inmate, Divanovich, was apparently having trouble getting over the fence and was apprehended. Officer Toney said in his statement, "I tried to tell Mr. Norris that there was two inmates and not just one, but no one would listen to me." The other escapee was likely Inmate Glen Blaylock, who would be apprehended within the hour.

Field Lieutenant Floyd McHan had gotten the escape call at his Eight Camp residence about two miles from the compound shortly before 10:00 p.m. After making the trip to the compound in record time, he was advised by Major Reed, his supervisor, to proceed to the dog kennel and get one of the several packs of dogs ready to go.

Chapter 8

Tracking Dogs

A pack of well-trained dogs with good handlers is the most important tool when it comes to tracking down escapees. Before the 1960s, pure-bred Bloodhounds were used. Bloodhounds are probably the best in the world when it comes to tracking humans, but there are some disadvantages to running only Bloodhounds. First, Bloodhounds generally must be leashed because they are hard to control and not apt to follow commands of the handler. Second, they do not run well in packs. A Bloodhound is intent on following the scent regardless of who or what is around him. They also do not tend to make much noise as they track; therefore, it is hard to know where the Bloodhound is and when the dog has found the subject.

By the 1970s, the Department's dog kennels were running packs of dogs with some Bloodhound mix in them, say 10 percent, but the majority was some type of hunting dog, perhaps a Bluetick or Black and Tan. The ears on these dogs are shorter which means that they tend to track more with their heads up. This makes it easier for them to run in packs. Plus, they make noise, lots of noise, which makes it easier for the handlers to follow them while on horseback.

The breeding and training of tracking dogs is a complex science. Once a breed has been chosen, then the training begins. A typical prison dog kennel will have a Dog Lieutenant and a lower ranking officer, and as many as five or six inmate dog handlers. The dogs begin their training within a few months of birth, and coaching continues for the rest of their lives. Every day a track is laid down by an inmate dog handler and dogs are turned loose to run the track. Some dogs take to it, while some don't. Some are easy to train; others are not. Dogs are rewarded and disciplined, and those that do not take well to training are culled from the pack and given away.

Probably the hardest struggle is to train a dog to track humans and not animals. Dogs naturally want to track game, especially deer. The handlers will intentionally train dogs in an area where there is other wildlife to coach them to follow the human scent and ignore the wildlife scent. Dogs that do not learn to track only human scents are culled from the team.

The dog crew may have as many as four packs at the ready, each with five to 10 dogs. One Pack would be the best tracking dogs and the pack that is chosen first for the chase. Two Pack would be the next best group of dogs, and so on. More than one pack is necessary to maintain because there may be times when multiple packs are needed, like on the night of January 1. There also may be chases that last for many hours, and fresh packs need to be at the ready to give the others a rest.

One other interesting misconception about tracking dogs is that many think that the dogs are aggressive and will attack their victim when tracked down. This is not the case. Dogs are not trained to be aggressive; they are taught to follow a scent. Many times they are used by local law enforcement agencies to track down lost children or senior citizens who are lost in a remote area. It would be a tragedy if the dogs were aggressive toward vulnerable individuals. Dogs may make a lot of noise, but once they find their subject, they are generally ready to play and will not bite or be aggressive unless provoked by the victim.

This may help explain one unusual event that happened the night of January 1. One of Tucker Prison's tracking dogs was found dead with its underbelly split open. It was surmised that one of the escapees caught the dog, killed it, and split it open to stick his hands or feet inside the animal so that he could warm his extremities.

Chapter 9

The Dogs Enter the Chase

When Lt. McHan arrived at the Dog Kennel, he loaded Two Pack on the truck and his saddled horse in a trailer pulled by the dog truck. He was instructed to go to Zone 5 on the perimeter of the compound near where Divonavich had gone over the fence and start a drag with the dogs. He and an inmate dog handler unloaded the horse and dogs on the south side of the compound and began looking for a scent. As McHan mounted his horse and began following the dogs, he noticed a figure walking toward the compound from the southwest. McHan told the dog handler to go ahead and follow the dogs and he would go check out the mysterious figure. As McHan approached the form, it turned out to be Inmate Glenn Blaylock, who was walking back toward the compound that he had just recently been so anxious to get away from. Years after the event, McHan recounted what Blaylock said to him as McHan approached him. He said, "Lock me up. Do whatever you want to do with me. Just get me where it's warm!" McHan had only one problem: he could hear radio traffic on his state-issued walkie-talkie, but for some reason, he could not transmit, which meant he could not alert officials that he had apprehended one of the escapees not far from the compound. The only solution he could think of was to walk Blaylock back to the unit and stand at the Laundry Gate on the south side of the compound until he could get someone's attention. This he did, and it was not long before one of the officers in the tower saw McHan with his prisoner standing outside the fence. Officials were alerted and several vehicles quickly converged on the area and Blaylock was taken back into the building. McHan again joined the chase with Two Pack which was running south of the compound in a westerly direction. The time was approximately 11:15 p.m. Two down, eight to go.

The official report filed by the Department states that Inmate Barney Norton went over the north fence around Zone 2. The evidence, however, points to the probability that Norton was one of three inmates who scaled the fence on the south side near the Laundry Gate in Zone 6. When questioned after the escape, Norton refused to make any statements regarding the escape, even refusing to admit that he ever left the East Building. It is likely that officials were mistaken as to where Norton scaled the fence. If Norton had gone over on the north side, he would have had to go east, then south, then west, all the while making a large circle around Cummins. Since he and Inmate Blaylock were caught in the same general vicinity and very close to the same time, it is reasonable to assume that Norton and Blaylock successfully made it over the south fence while Inmate Divanovich was slightly behind them, had trouble getting over the fence, and was caught while coming down on the outside of the fence.

Norton was following roughly the same route he had used in his previous escape in 1978. He was headed toward the highway, not toward the river where most of the other escapees were heading. Norton made it to a field that was just over a mile from the compound, less than a quarter mile from Highway 388 and about a mile from Highway 65. As he heard the dogs from One Pack approaching, he laid down on his stomach in some tall grass that surrounded a utility pole at the perimeter of the field. The dogs approached Norton, followed closely by Dog Lieutenant Harry D. Rhodes, Field Captain Winfred Ashcraft, and an inmate dog handler, all on horseback. Norton was ordered to stand up and put his hands on top of his head. He looked toward Rhodes, grinned, and said, "You have got me. I'm caught." Rhodes ordered Norton to step slowly away from the pole. After a few feet, he was ordered to stop, but he kept walking toward his captors. Rhodes then fired a warning shot in the air and Norton hit the ground so fast that Ashcraft at first thought that Rhodes had shot Norton. As Norton lay on his stomach on the ground, he was secured with zip ties and the compound was notified that one of the escapees was in custody. After a short time, Coleman Knight and Red Shadwick, both of whom worked on the farm, showed up in a vehicle to transport Norton back to the building. The time was approximately 11:15 p.m. Three down, seven to go.

It is interesting that Rhodes reported that Norton smiled when he was caught. A very similar scenario was reported by Major Dale Reed when Norton had escaped a few months earlier. Reed said that when the dogs tracked Norton down, he was standing in a slough. Reed and the dog handler were on horses and as Reed approached Norton, Norton turned toward Reed and smiled and said something like "Everything's going to be all right, Major." Reed said that the comment unnerved him a bit and he thought that there might be someone behind him who was going to assist Norton. It was as though Norton received some sort of adrenaline rush from the cat and mouse game.

Chapter 10

Two Groups of Three

Van Myers had a rough night that night. He worked at Cummins as a farm supervisor, overseeing about 2,000 acres of row crops on Unit One which is generally on the southeast part of the Cummins farm. He was a jovial man who had a smile that lit up his whole face and a laugh that was infectious. After four years on the farm, he probably knew it as well or better than any other employee. He knew every field, every turn row, and every drainage ditch. His knowledge of the farm would prove invaluable.

When Myers first got to Cummins that night, he was woefully unprepared. The heater did not work in his Dodge farm truck, and he did not have on nearly enough clothes, which necessitated a trip back home to get more. He not only got warmer clothes for himself but also for Building Lieutenant Jimmy Dougan, who was riding with him that night.

Along with patrolling in his vehicle, Myers was also tasked from time to time with getting a tractor from the Unit One shop to pull out trucks and trailers that periodically got mired down in the mud of the turn rows on the farm. When not on a tractor, he and Dougan patrolled on the east and south part of the farm, roughly from the Arkansas River levee to Nineteen Canal, which is near the southeast property line of Cummins. As they were slowly driving and looking, they spotted two individuals standing in the road near the Hole-in-the-Wall Bridge about 4:30 a.m. The Hole-in-the-Wall bridge is about two miles southeast of the compound. The two people turned out to be Inmates Ronnie Briggs and Terry Howell. Myers and Dougan learned that there was a third escapee, Inmate Jerry McKee, who was hiding in the grass near the road about 100 yards away. Apparently, McKee was so cold that he could hardly walk. By the time he came out of cover, the dog crew from Tucker had arrived on the scene and Lt. Waggoner and one of the inmate dog handlers assisted McKee in walking to where the others were standing. Mr. Myers radioed Mr. Lockhart and advised him that three had been apprehended. Warden Jerry Campbell and CID Investigator Jack Ursery soon showed up to transport the three back to the compound. This was approximately 4:30 a.m. Six down, four to go.

When Briggs, McKee, and Howell were returned to the compound, the clothing they had on was inventoried. Inmate Briggs was wearing the uniform pants and shirt of Officer Moon. While he had on thermal underwear, no coat was mentioned. Inmate McKee had on white pants, gloves, and a field jacket, but no shirt. Inmate Howell was dressed the warmest of the three with thermals, white pants and shirt, and two field jackets. All three had on state brogans. Their inadequate clothing may explain why Briggs and Howell were standing on a road in plain view of Myers and Dougan. They may have wanted to be apprehended.

Warden Campbell, with Director Jim Mabry's blessing, also ordered that the three be shaved and given haircuts when they returned to the compound. During this time, it was a rule that inmates were to wear short hair and no facial hair. Several inmates, including Briggs, McKee, and Howell, had taken the "vow of the Nazarite," patterned after the vow that Samson took in the Old Testament. Part of that oath meant that no razor would touch the hair or beard of the one taking the vow. While it was general knowledge that this was just a ruse by the inmates to be able to grow long hair, about a half dozen inmates had been growing their hair and beards long and had filed a motion in federal court seeking an exemption to the grooming rule based on a sincerely held religious belief. The judge had not yet ruled on the motion, but the inmates were holding on to their right to wear hair long and let their beards grow and refused to conform to the Department's grooming policy.

The decision to cut the long hair and shave these three inmates was ostensibly made for security reasons. They were rephotographed after the haircuts and shaves. Officials indicated that the inmates would be easier to identify if they were free of long hair and facial hair. The decision to shave the hair and beards of these inmates would become a problem for officials when they tried to explain their actions in federal court several months later.

Approximately 30 minutes after Myers and Dougan caught the three escapees, they radioed the Armory Tower and asked for a unit to relieve them so they could go somewhere and warm up. A relief vehicle was dispatched, but before Myers and Dougan could make it back to the compound, they were once again called to get a tractor and pull out another stuck truck and trailer. This they did, and finally made it back to the compound and warmed up for about 20 minutes. The temperature had dropped to the single digits and the wind was 12 to 15 miles an hour. The chill factor was well below zero.

By the time Myers and Dougan resumed their patrol near the Hole-in-the-Wall bridge, daylight was approaching. They were looking for any sign that might indicate that the four remaining escapees were in the area. At approximately 7:45 a.m., Myers noticed something in a field that caught his attention. When he emerged from the vehicle and walked out into the field to investigate, he found what he believed to be tracks of at least three people. He radioed Warden Campbell of the discovery and the dog unit from Tucker Prison was dispatched to the location. Field Captain Harold Chadick and Lieutenant Waggoner, along with an inmate dog handler, put the pack of dogs out at the tracks and they immediately struck a scent and started running east. Along the way, the dogs discovered two places where the inmates had apparently stopped to rest. The officers found bits of clothing along with other signs of disturbance. As the dogs neared the eastern boundary of the Cummins property, they began acting as though they were near the subjects. Chadick and Waggoner then caught sight of three inmates hiding in a brush pile. They were given an order to come out, which they did. As they emerged, Chadick and Waggoner observed that two of the inmates, Ronnie Pucilowski and Gary Morse, had no shoes on, while Inmate Johnny Wiggins had on a pair of state brogans. Whatever footwear the two had at the beginning of the escape had been lost as they made their way across the mud and mire of the terrain. They had gone approximately two and a half miles southeast of the compound, no more than a mile from where Briggs, Howell, and McKee were apprehended. Lockhart was notified by radio that the three had been caught and Warden Campbell and Captain Johnny King were dispatched to pick them up. The time was approximately 8:30 a.m. Nine down, one to go.

As with the other escapees, Pucilowski, Morse, and Wiggins were transported to Sally Port Gate and then walked into the prison. There is a photograph of Pucilowski and Wiggins on the front page of the *Arkansas Gazette* on Wednesday, January 3, 1979, as they were being led back into the prison through the Sally Port Gate. Witnesses at the time said that as Pucilowski walked, his foot sounded like a rock hitting the concrete every time he took a step because his feet were so frozen.

Instead of being taken directly to the East Building, the three were taken to the infirmary due to the severe frostbite they suffered. Infirmary personnel soaked their feet in lukewarm water. Because Inmate Wiggins was wearing brogans at the time of his capture, his frostbite was minimal, and he was soon returned to the East Building. Pucilowski and Morse, however, experienced severe frostbite to their feet and were transported to Jefferson County Hospital in Pine Bluff, where they remained until February 23, 1979. Upon being returned to Cummins, they remained on the infirmary ward until authorized by the prison physician, Dr. Carl Adams, and the attending physician from the hospital, Dr. Raymond Irwin.

Because of the frostbite, three toes were surgically amputated from Pucilowski. He lost both great toes, and the distal tip of the second digit on the right foot. Morse had tissue removed from the frostbitten area but did not lose any toes.

Apparently, there was some question as to why the two spent so long in Jefferson Hospital. In a memo from John Byus, Supervisor of Medical Services for the Department, to A. L. Lockhart, Asst. Director, dated February 28, 1979, Byus states, "There has been much speculation as to why both had been on the verge of release at an earlier date only to have them remain in Jefferson County Hospital. On two occasions, my office received reports from Chief of Hospital Security, Sergeant Sylvester Tillman, that Dr. Irwin had established a minimum release date for Morse and Pucilowski. As this period approached it was extended due to unforeseeable changes relative to their condition. As with any frostbite victim, no exact time period can be expected, and surgical procedures are utilized as last resort allowing all possibility of tissue regeneration."

Chapter 11

And Then There Was One

Of all the poor planning done that fateful night, Inmate Jerome Bargo probably did the best poor planning of all the escapees. It is evident that the strategy of all the escapees got no further than getting over the fence and running. There was no plan to meet anywhere. There was no one on the outside to pick up the inmates once they were free of the compound. Apparently, the only objective was to get over the fence, run, and hope for the best.

If running was the plan, then Bargo was best prepared, even though "best" is a relative term. He had gotten word a day or two before that something was going down on New Year's night. He came to the dayroom that night with a pair of socks in his pocket and a razor blade and fingernail clippers secreted on his person. When the door was popped and the East Building was under the control of the inmates, Bargo left the dayroom and went to the clothing room and got a pair of brogans, a coat, and a toboggan. He then went to the Control Room where he got a towel and pressed it to Officer Bryant's head to try to stop the bleeding, eventually changing the handcuffs from behind Bryant's back to the front so that the officer could hold the towel to his head. After escorting Bryant back to Cell #12 with the rest of the officers, Bargo left the building and made his way to the fence.

The favored place to go over the fence on the north side was at the Construction Gate because the barbed wire at the top was easier to get over, but there was a problem. Bargo saw a line of about four inmates waiting to go over and the first one was struggling to place a laundry bag over the top to make it easier for the others to scale the fence without getting hung up in the barbed wire. Bargo ran down to another section of the fence and scaled it as fast as he could. As his feet hit the ground on the outside, Officer Melvin Wiley cut loose with his AR-15 from the Sally Port Tower. Bargo started running east away from the compound as fast as he could.

Bargo was no stranger to running. His official Cummins record indicated that he had three escapes, one in Arkansas, one in Kentucky, and one in Virginia. This was only half the story. According to Bargo, he had escaped three times from juvenile facilities, starting at the age of 13, two times from county facilities, and once, just two months prior to the January 1 incident, from Cummins.

The reason that Bargo was in the East Building on maximum security status was an escape on October 30, 1978, in which he was involved. Bargo, along with Inmates John "Big Time" Oliver, David Bosnick, Floyd Meneley, and Gary Morse had made their way down the West Hall of Cummins and out the West Hall door, then through the Blood Bank and out the back door and over the fence that was only a few feet from the back door of the Blood Bank. All this was accomplished because Inmate Oliver had been able to secure keys to the West Hall door and the Blood Bank.

During that escape, Bargo had been the first to be caught. He made it about three miles to the Arkansas River levee before being apprehended as he was hiding in some back water. Two others, Oliver and Bosnick, made it a little farther down the levee before being caught. Morse and Meneley enjoyed a few more days of freedom before being apprehended.

On the night of January 1, Bargo knew that he had to keep running, had to stay warm, and had to do this on his own, not joining up with other inmates as they sped away from the compound. In an interview, Bargo said that he made it to the Arkansas River, but more than likely he made it to Douglas Lake, about two miles from Cummins. Douglas Lake was once part of the river channel, but over the course of time, as natural events occurred, the river was rerouted and the cut off portion became a lake. The lake is on the river side of the levee, which may have made Bargo think he was looking at the Arkansas River.

After following the levee for a short distance, Bargo cut south and headed in the general direction of the small town of Gould, which is about five miles from Cummins. He ran for most of the night. His shoes were caked with ice and as he ran through wet areas, his pant legs froze from about the knee down. Just as the sky was beginning to lighten at the crack of dawn, Bargo saw a light in the distance. He figured it was a house and there would possibly be a car to steal or a place he could hide and get warm. As he approached the house, he saw that it was a farming operation with an equipment shed out back of the farmer's house. The shed was open on the sides and sheltered some tractors and other equipment from the weather. Luckily, the tractors had closed cabs.

Bargo believed this would be an excellent place to hide during the daylight hours. It was an open shed, so if authorities showed up, maybe they would not try to shake it down since just about everything was visible from the outside. He climbed into a tractor cab, grabbed some feed sacks, cut off his frozen pant legs from the knee down with his razorblade, took off his brogans, and wrapped the feed sacks around his lower legs and feet. The tractor even had an FM radio, and he was able to tune in to the local news and learn that all but four of the escapees had been caught.

Bargo hid in the cab for several hours, being careful to wiggle his toes and move as much as he could to keep warm. His luck would not hold out, however, because about 9:30 or 10:00 a.m., he heard the back door of the house slam and saw the farmer coming out to the equipment shed. Little did he know that this farmer was particular about his equipment and during the cold weather, he made it a practice to go out each day to start the equipment and let it warm up a bit.

When the farmer got to the tractor in which Bargo was hiding, he opened the cab door, saw Bargo, and both were startled. The farmer had been watching the news and knew of the escapes, and when he saw Bargo, he quickly concluded that one of the fugitives was hiding in his tractor. He got down in a hurry and retreated to the house to notify authorities.

Bargo figured that the end was near, but he put on his brogans, got down from the cab, and started running away from the shed and the house. He had no interest in going after the farmer or doing him harm. He noticed a clump of trees off in the distance and knew this might be his only chance. All the land around the farmer's house was open fields and there was no place to hide.

As Bargo approached the trees, he saw what appeared to be an old, abandoned house. Even though he knew that he would be found, he figured the house was his only chance. When he went in, he noticed an opening to the attic that was covered by a hatch. The opening was at least eight feet off the floor and not easily accessible except with a ladder. Bargo discovered that if he could run and bounce off the wall, he had a chance of grabbing hold of the attic opening. After several tries, he was able to take hold of the opening and shimmy his way into the attic. He was safe for the moment.

When the authorities got the call that the last escapee had been spotted, it was all hands on deck. Two packs of dogs converged on the location as well as a plethora of officers, and even a few of the media. The dogs ran the track from the farmer's equipment shed to the abandoned house. As authorities approached the house, someone yelled out on a megaphone, "Come on out, Bargo, we know you're in there." This unnerved Bargo. How did they know it was him? At last account, he had heard there were four escapees still out. Bargo did not know the others had been caught and he was the last fugitive.

The officials went in and shook down the house. They saw the hatch to the attic, but since it was so high, and they didn't have a ladder, they did not attempt to go into the attic. They went back out and attempted to get the dogs to pick up a scent that would indicate that Bargo went past the abandoned house and kept running. The dogs kept coming back to the abandoned house.

Finally, Bargo heard someone yell from the outside, "Tear this son-of-a-bitch down if you have to. He's in there somewhere." The shakedown got serious. It wasn't long before Bargo saw a head pop up through the attic opening. He was spotted and given the order to come down, which he did. As Bargo was led away from the house, there were several cameras from the media present. Bargo always thought that the light treatment he got during his capture was due to several outside witnesses being at the location when he was apprehended. The time was approximately 12:00 Noon. Ten down, none to go.

Lockhart and Ursery transported Bargo back to the compound. Bargo related that as they were traveling back to the compound, Lockhart turned to him and said, "You know you got an

64

ass whipping coming when you get back." Bargo answered in the affirmative, but the ass whipping never came. As a matter of fact, Bargo indicated that in all his time in the Department of Corrections, no one ever laid a hand on him.

Chapter 12

High Fives All Around

A small miracle had just happened. A major disturbance in a maximum security facility, involving inmates who had committed some of the most reprehensible crimes in Arkansas, had been quelled within an hour of when it started. Ten inmates, most of whom were skilled at escaping from incarceration, had been apprehended within 14 hours of their escape. No one from the public had been harmed. No cars had been stolen. No houses had been broken into and no damage had been done. It was a masterful effort involving more than a hundred individuals from local law enforcement, the state police, and personnel from the Department of Corrections. It also involved men on horseback, at least three packs of dogs, and even a state police airplane that aided in tracking down Bargo.

The minutes of the January 25 Board of Corrections Meeting reflect that Chairman Richard Earl Griffin wanted "to express to the Department of Corrections and to the staff and asked those staff present to notify the officers involved in the escape attempts on January 1, that many of the Board were personally present that night and the Board knows of the adverse circumstances and conditions that existed and the Board feels that the staff reacted in a most admirable way. The employees and staff were on duty for 36 hours without rest. Some were on horseback in weather that was nine degrees with 20 and 30 knot winds and a chill factor of about 30 below, and the personnel stayed with it even when the dogs would not get out of the trucks to run. All personnel reacted admirably. The Department does a remarkable job of catching escapees. Enough cannot be said for the men who work with dogs. The dogs are trained well…. The Board knows and appreciated what Mr. Lockhart and his employees did when faced with the problem of six officers held as hostages. One officer required medical attention, and a few inmates received minor injuries. The quality and skill shown in keeping the situation under control is appreciated."

There was one person who led and coordinated all the efforts of that night, Assistant Director A. L. "Art" Lockhart. Standing at six feet six inches tall, he was known by many as "The Tall Man." He was one of those people who was a commanding presence when he walked into the room. He was intimidating, and he used that to his advantage. He sometimes would point his "45 caliber" finger at someone and say, "Friend, let me tell you something!" From that point on, one knew that he was about to get dressed down in royal fashion.

Lockhart lived and breathed corrections. As a former warden of Cummins, he knew the lay of the land as well as anyone. He also had something else in his favor: he had a mind that could quickly process information, develop a plan, and place personnel, pack dogs, and equipment where they were needed to maximize the search efforts. Once he placed someone at a designated place, he expected them to stay there until he moved them, and he never forgot where anyone was placed. He was probably the best in the country at running an escape. Unfortunately, since moving to Arkansas almost a decade before, he had had plenty of practice. It was a common occurrence for inmates to run off from work details or climb over a fence that was inadequate to stop inmates who were determined to run. There were far too few correctional officers, and this was long before lethal fences, rolls and rolls of concertina wire (commonly mispronounced as "constantine" wire), and microwave detectors along the perimeter. In 1979, it was just the wits of the inmates matched against the wits of the authorities, and there was no better commander-in-chief than Art Lockhart.

If, on January 2, 1979, at 12:00 noon, the inmates had been locked back in their cells, and all the officers had left and gone to a local bar, had a drink, and toasted their success, this would have been heralded as one of the most astounding feats in the history of corrections. Unfortunately, the events that happened inside the East Building after the disturbance was quelled and the escapees returned would taint the tremendous success of those 14 fateful hours.

Chapter 13

Silence Is Golden...Almost

Jack Ursery was a criminal investigator for the Arkansas State Police. He was assigned to the Department of Corrections to investigate incidences within the agency. He was present from the takeover of the East Building until the last escapee was apprehended. As a matter of fact, he and Lockhart were the ones who drove Inmate Jerome Bargo, the last escapee to be caught, back to Cummins at noon on January 2. Ursery was given the monumental task of compiling an investigative report that started when Inmate Johnny Wiggins struck the blow on Officer Bryant's head at approximately 9:45 p.m., January 1, 1979, until August 26, 1980, when the final status report was filed listing the convictions of those who were involved in the takeover and escape.

Ursery did a masterful job of collecting detailed information. His report was over 350 pages. It included written witness statements, personal interviews with inmates and officers, and the charges that were filed and disposition of those charges, along with diagrams and other pertinent data that illuminated what went on that fateful night.

When one reads all the official statements written by officers and administrative officials regarding the events of that night that were entered into the CID investigative report, there is no mention of any physical force being used, or needing to be used, by officials. In his investigator notes written on January 4, 1979, Ursery made this statement regarding the retaking of the East Building by officers, "Officers then armed with riot sticks, shotguns, and rifles, secured each wing without incident, locking down inmates in their cells." Farther down in the report when writing about apprehending Inmate Willie Brown who had hidden in the quiet cell on the South Wing of the East Building, Ursery wrote, "Brown was taken by officers, handcuffed, moved to the front portion of the building, and placed back in his cell, without incident."

In addition to Ursery's report, there is a statement in the official press release prepared by Tim Baltz, Public Information Officer for the Department, which reads, "Total control of the building (East Building) was regained by the officers at approximately 10:15 p.m. There were no confrontations between officers and the inmates in the building once they entered the Control Area and seized control." There is no mention of physical force being used during or after the takeover.

On January 4–5, 1979, Ursery interviewed inmates who did not escape, but participated in the takeover of the East Building. These included Inmates Charles Pickens, Charles Neal, Willie Brown, Earl Van Denton, Paul Ruiz, and Curtis Austin. Most answered Ursery's questions and cooperated. Only Willie Brown indicated that he did not want to answer any questions before talking to an attorney. None of these inmates mentioned any use of physical force by officers on the night of January 1 or early morning of January 2.

Ursery also interviewed all the escapees on January 4–5. Most refused to answer any questions about the incident, invoking their right to remain silent. Those refusing to answer questions included Inmates Ismet Divanovich, Glenn Blaylock, Ronnie Briggs, Jerry McKee, Gary Morse, Terry Howell, and Ronnie Pucilowski. On the other hand, Jerome Bargo gave a lengthy account of that night, with his witness statement running 11 pages. Johnnie Wiggins gave a six-page account, even talking about striking Officer Bryant at the beginning of the takeover. None of the escapees spoke of any physical force being used by officers at any time during the night of January 1 or early morning of January 2.

Of all the freeworld personnel and inmates who wrote statements or were interviewed for the CID report, only Inmate Barney Norton spoke of physical force being used. When interviewed by Ursery, Norton was asked what was wrong. He replied, "I've been beat to death, Mr. Ursery. I believe physical evidence speaks for itself." When asked what happened, Norton replied, "There is an officer that nearly beat me to death, Mr. K. Taylor."

The exchange between Norton and Ursery, along with Asst. Warden Larry Norris, is interesting. A significant portion of the conversation is quoted below:

NORTON: What evidence of a crime do you have to have to issue a warrant to make an arrest?

URSERY: That will be up to the prosecuting attorney.

NORTON: I'm talking about you yourself, if you witness a crime. What evidence would you have to have to make an arrest?

URSERY: It would be up to the prosecuting attorney. I didn't arrest you, I'm not arresting you now.

NORTON: I'm not asking that. As a State Policeman, I would like for you to place a man here under arrest for assault on my life and he intended to kill me.

URSERY: Well, I cannot make arrests on anybody's say so. You go to the prosecuting attorney and present the facts to him and if he sees fit, he will investigate it.

NORTON: How do I go about doing that?

URSERY: Well, you have to contact the prosecuting attorney's office.

NORTON: Have you got his name?

URSERY: Wayne Matthews.

NORTON: Pine Bluff?

URSERY: Pine Bluff. No problem at all.

NORTON: Mr. Norris, you're the superintendent here. I would like to tell you that I need medical attention bad. I've got a busted eardrum, the doctor confirmed that yesterday. I'm coughing up a big glob of blood back there in my cell too.

NORRIS: When was the last time you saw a doctor Barney?

NORTON: Monday sometime during the day.

URSERY: Monday, January 1?

NORTON: Monday or Tuesday, I'm not sure.

URSERY: Was it before or after you ran off Barney?

NORTON: I don't know that I run off Mr. Ursery. It was after Mr. Taylor beat me up.

URSERY: Do you know who brought you back to the institution Barney?

NORTON: I have no idea. I don't even know that I left the institution.

URSERY: I just wondered how you got over the barbed wire fence and 3 rolls of wire.

NORTON: Did you see me do this?

URSERY: Did not see you do this. Just simply what I've been told.

NORTON: I would like to state to you Mr. Ursery as a member of the Arkansas State Police, that I do have 3 witnesses present here in the East Building at this time that heard Mr. Taylor threaten to kill me before I got to the room where the man beat me and after I got out of the room after he beat me. He told me he was going to collect the money to put up on my life out of Little Rock right to my face right there in the Dayroom. The man told me he had been waiting for this chance to kill me and he tried to beat me to death. He broke two night sticks on me and possibly a third. Two men were holding shotguns.

In all the witness statements and transcripts of interviews in Ursery's criminal investigation report, this is the only allegation of physical force being used that night. According to an article in the *Arkansas Democrat* on April 6, 1979, it was confirmed that Ursery did relate Norton's allegation of a beating to Prosecuting Attorney Wayne Matthews, but Matthews did not follow up on it. Matthews is quoted as saying, "I never did hear anything else about it." He continued, "What is excessive force under Correction Department regulations or under the federal court order may not be excessive force under Arkansas criminal statute."

While there is nothing in the CID investigation about physical force being used, other than the instances mentioned, there were some written statements in the January *Monthly Report to the Board of Correction* indicating that physical force was used. It was the policy at that time that any use of mace, gas, or physical force used by officers was submitted to the Board via a written report and the reports became a part of the permanent record of Board proceedings. Four reports, all dated January 2, involving seven inmates, were submitted. The contents of these reports will be discussed in subsequent chapters.

Chapter 14

Setting the Stage for
a Compliance Coordinator

If one is to understand how the incident of January 1 was to become a fulcrum, or perfect storm, that would influence corrections for decades to come, one must understand the role of the federal courts in molding and shaping prison reform beginning in the late 1960s. For a detailed, scholarly account of how federal courts influenced reform in Arkansas prisons, Dr. Mary Parker's doctoral dissertation, "Judicial Intervention in Correctional Institutions: The Arkansas Odyssey," is the magnum opus. Her dissertation was completed in 1986 and was written to fulfill her requirements for a PhD from Sam Houston University, Huntsville, Texas. It is a 400-page research document that chronicles how federal courts got involved in and shaped prison reform in Arkansas. The account in this writing will be brief and will lean heavily on the masterful research done by Dr. Parker.

Before the 1960s federal courts generally had a "hands off" attitude toward prisons. The common thought was that prisoners did something bad to end up in prison and whatever treatment they got, they largely deserved. It was believed that prisoners, for the most part, gave up their rights when they were confined to prison. They were viewed more like slaves than citizens.

In the late 1960s the view of the federal courts started changing. The courts began looking at prisoners more like citizens than slaves. The courts began ruling on more lawsuits from prisoners that alleged that constitutional rights of prisoners had been violated.

In the late 1960s and throughout the 1970s, there was a series of lawsuits filed by Arkansas prisoners alleging that conditions within the Arkansas Department of Corrections were unconstitutional. The first one of significance was Holt v. Sarver in June 1969. The inmates who filed the lawsuit listed several issues that they felt represented unconstitutional conditions. Two of six issues were determined to be constitutionally deficient by the court: first, the State had failed to provide a system that protected inmates from violent assault and second, the general conditions of the isolation cells were inhumane.

The first issue stemmed from prisoners being confined in large, open barracks without the benefit of proper supervision, thus allowing inmates to prey on each other. The second issue came from the obvious deficiency of isolation cells. The punitive isolation area at Cummins was horrific. As many as 11 prisoners were confined in a small cell. Toilets did not work properly. Prisoners shared bedding, which propagated disease. It was an inhumane experience to be locked up in punitive isolation.

Although there were only two issues in that first lawsuit, subsequent lawsuits began to expose other areas of concern by the courts, including overcrowding, medical and dental care, rehabilitation programs, mail and visitation, inmate safety, race relations and discrimination, grievance procedures, brutality, and disciplinary issues, to name a few.

By the late 1970s there was a well-worn path to and from the Department, the Attorney General's office, and Judge G. Thomas Eisele's courtroom in Little Rock. Officials from the Department were required to make regular reports on the progress made in conforming to the edicts of the Court. Sometimes it was noted that sufficient progress was being made, sometimes not.

By 1978, there was discussion between the parties about a possible compromise agreement that would culminate in the settlement of the disputed issues and bring the Department into constitutional status. The first hint of a compromise came out in late June. Judge Eisele issued guidelines to reform the inmate disciplinary process on June 30. His remarks were primarily aimed at practices that went on while Mike Hawke was warden at Cummins a year earlier. A former disciplinary chairman, Ross Martin, testified that he sometimes was told how to rule on certain disciplinaries before the actual disciplinary hearing. He stated that the warden and two assistant wardens would intervene in certain disciplinary cases and express the punishment that would be administered before the disciplinary court heard the evidence.

Judge Eisele's remarks, while talking about events that happened a year earlier, are strangely prophetic. In his 34-page order, he included the remarks, "When arrogant, unprincipled, and evil men are in control, the rule of law becomes meaningless. Having no respect for the law or the rights of others, they quickly devise schemes to 'get around' these barriers to the imposition of their own wills." Eisele went on to say, "Evil men do find their way into positions of power and then operate contrary to their employers' own rules and regulations, and indeed, unlawfully."

When Director Jim Mabry was questioned by *Associated Press* reporter, Bill Simmons, a few days after the ruling, Mabry said that the Department would "dot every 'i' and cross every 't'" when it came to complying with the order the judge issued on disciplinary procedures. Mabry is quoted as saying, "The laws are what the courts say they are and we're going to do what he says do—I'd like to even go beyond that and more, but at least we certainly don't intend to drag our feet."

At its August meeting, the Board of Corrections voted to settle the lawsuits brought by inmates over the past decade. They would make known their intentions to seek settlement before the next hearing set by Eisele on September 5. While the Board was anxious to end the litigation, they were hesitant to give the compliance coordinator, a new position created to oversee the agreement, too much power. There was much discussion and a lot of modification on the proposed powers of the newly created position. Attorney General Bill Clinton assisted the Board in developing language that was suitable to the Board.

Because the decree stipulated that a new position would be created, that of a compliance coordinator, the Board's action had to be approved by the Legislative Council. Approval was given on September 1, which paved the way for the signing of the consent decree with a path of ending 10 years of intervention by the federal courts.

The consent decree was signed by all parties and approved by the Court on October 5, 1978. It called for the Department to come into compliance in 39 specific areas. These ranged from the prohibition of physical and verbal abuse of inmates by staff to no longer serving grue to inmates on isolation.

Along with the decree came the necessity to hire a compliance coordinator who would monitor the compliance of the Department with the consent decree and make regular reports to the Court as to the Department's compliance. The compliance coordinator could go wherever he wanted, whenever he wanted, talk to whomever he wanted, and examine any records of his choosing. He was to be given great latitude within the Department.

Chapter 15

Enter Stephen La Plante, Stage Left

A nation-wide search was undertaken to find a suitable compliance coordinator. There were 30 applicants for the job, with eight being called in for an interview. Of the finalists, Stephen La Plante from San Francisco, California, was chosen. La Plante was 30 years old and had been an ombudsman for the San Francisco jails for three and a half years. He had a bachelor's degree in sociology from the University of San Francisco and a master's degree in sociology from the University of Chicago. He left his $21,000 job in San Francisco to begin a $25,000 job as compliance coordinator on December 4, 1978. From the very beginning, La Plante had some tough issues with which to deal. He was from the west coast. His degrees were in sociology. He was moving into a culture that eyed people like him with great suspicion and distrust. Likewise, La Plante did not fully understand the culture into which he was moving and did not accept some of the tenets of that culture.

What were some of those tenets? In 1979 many of the rank-and-file officers within the Department adhered to some basic principles that were common in the Southern culture. During their interviews, officers spoke of having to "have that stuff" if they were to survive in the Department. What was "that stuff"? It meant that one would not back down from a fight and would run toward an altercation, not away from it. It meant that many disturbances were handled with fisticuffs. It was common for officers to fight even among themselves. Officers were known to "go across the levee" to settle a dispute.

So even though the very first item of the consent decree read, "No Arkansas Department of Corrections employee will use excessive force against any inmate," it did not mean that "head thumping," as it was commonly called, immediately ceased. The use of force ran deep in the warp and weft of the culture of maintaining order within the prison. It was pretty much an accepted fact that if an inmate assaulted an officer, or escaped from the prison, he would receive a "head thumping" as part of the retribution for the actions. While these actions were generally carried out by officers in uniform, they were tacitly overlooked, if not clandestinely encouraged, by upper-level management.

In addition to the first item, there was another item in the decree that dealt with excessive force. Item 30 read, "Allegations of excessive force against inmates by ADC employees will be formally investigated at once and reduced to writing by the ADC and will include the inmate's version of the incident." While it could be argued that ADC officials did not define the force used on January 1-2 as excessive, it is clear that Inmate Barney Norton made an allegation of excessive physical force against Captain Kenny Taylor when Norton was interviewed by CID Investigator Jack Ursery and Assistant Warden Larry Norris on January 4.

The perfect storm was about to explode. An officer had been assaulted. A maximum-security unit had been hijacked. Officers were taken hostage. Inmates escaped. And not just any inmates. These were some of the most reprehensible, belligerent, rebellious, trouble-causing inmates in the Department. Someone was going to have to pay.

Even if one paints the very best picture on what happened and lists all the justifications one can, many of the actions of that night are still totally unjustifiable. Perhaps there were a few instances when inmates might have been perceived to put up some resistance, thus justifying physical force, but a reasonable person would conclude that much of what went on that night was unwarranted and inexcusable.

Chapter 16

Blood On the Walls

In one of Richard Pryor's comedy routines, he relates a story about being caught by his wife with another woman. He turns to his wife and asks the question, "Who you gonna believe? Me? Or your lying eyes?"

The truth of that night is hard to establish because of the totally divergent accounts narrated by the officers and the inmates. An attempt will be made to give a well-balanced view of the events, and the reader can determine if the pendulum of truth swings more toward the inmates or the officers.

One fact that can be established: there was blood in the East Building that night and apparently lots of it. The blood was not there during the time that inmates were in control of the East Building (except for Officer Bryant's head wound when he was hit by Inmate Wiggins during the initial takeover), nor during the take back of the building by officers. The bloodletting happened after the building had been secured and the officers were in charge. Several witnesses refer to the blood. There was blood in the lobby, the dayroom, and the bathroom. Infirmary Administrator Billy Abbott spoke of seeing blood as he entered the East Building to start tending to inmates who were injured and bleeding. Inmate Chester Treadwell, an infirmary worker who was sent out to help Abbott, spoke of the presence of blood in the building. Inmate Jerome Bargo mentioned seeing blood in the building after he was returned from escape the next day.

So, how did so much blood end up in the East Building that night? That was the subject of Stephen La Plante's first report after coming to the job of compliance coordinator. La Plante sort of stumbled into the possibility that excessive force might have been used during the events of January 1 and 2. He had traveled to Cummins on Thursday, January 4, to talk to inmates about complaints that had been filed about the mail service. He entered the East Building in the late afternoon to interview some of the inmates assigned there. The first inmate he spoke with was Inmate Ronnie Briggs. During the course of the interview, Briggs showed La Plante numerous lacerations and indicated several employees had beat him after he was returned to the East Building after escaping. Briggs told La Plante there were other inmates who had been victims of excessive force the night of the escape.

La Plante spent about two hours that night interviewing various inmates about the incident. The next day, on January 5, La Plante met with Director Jim Mabry for two hours about what he found and suggested to Mabry that there should be a "joint investigation" by the compliance coordinator and someone from the administration of the Department chosen by Mabry to assist in the investigation. Mabry chose George Brewer, Assistant to the Director, to assist La Plante in the investigation.

Brewer was probably less than excited to be selected by Mabry to become co-investigator with La Plante so that it could be viewed as a "joint investigation." Brewer would have the arduous task of investigating individuals with whom he had worked, and sometimes worked under, for six years. But Brewer was probably the best choice for the job. For one thing, he was recognized as having one of the sharpest minds in the Department. For another, he was perceived as being fair. He reminded one of Mr. Spock on *Star Trek*. Brewer had a logical mind. He tended to stick with the facts and go wherever the facts and the truth led him. This is not to say that he had no trepidation as he entered the investigation.

La Plante, along with Brewer, conducted a thorough investigation of the incident. They interviewed and obtained witness statements from all relevant parties. They examined infirmary records. Photographs were taken of the injuries. La Plante requested that many of the players take polygraph tests. All the inmates agreed to the polygraphs, but most of the officers refused and were eventually disciplined for not cooperating. By the time the report was complete, there would be 11 inmate complainants and 16 accused employees. Thirty employees would be interviewed, along with 14 inmates.

The inmates alleged that employees of the Arkansas Department of Corrections "assaulted them in excess of any justified force to subdue them." They further alleged that they were beaten with batons, slappers, butts of weapons, as well as hands and feet of employees.

Photographs and Diagrams

Looking east from the Armory Tower. This is roughly the view the officer would have had toward where the inmates went over the fence on the night of the escape. This photo was taken in 1985 and the tall outer fence was not erected in 1979.

All photographs in this section were taken by the author in 1985.

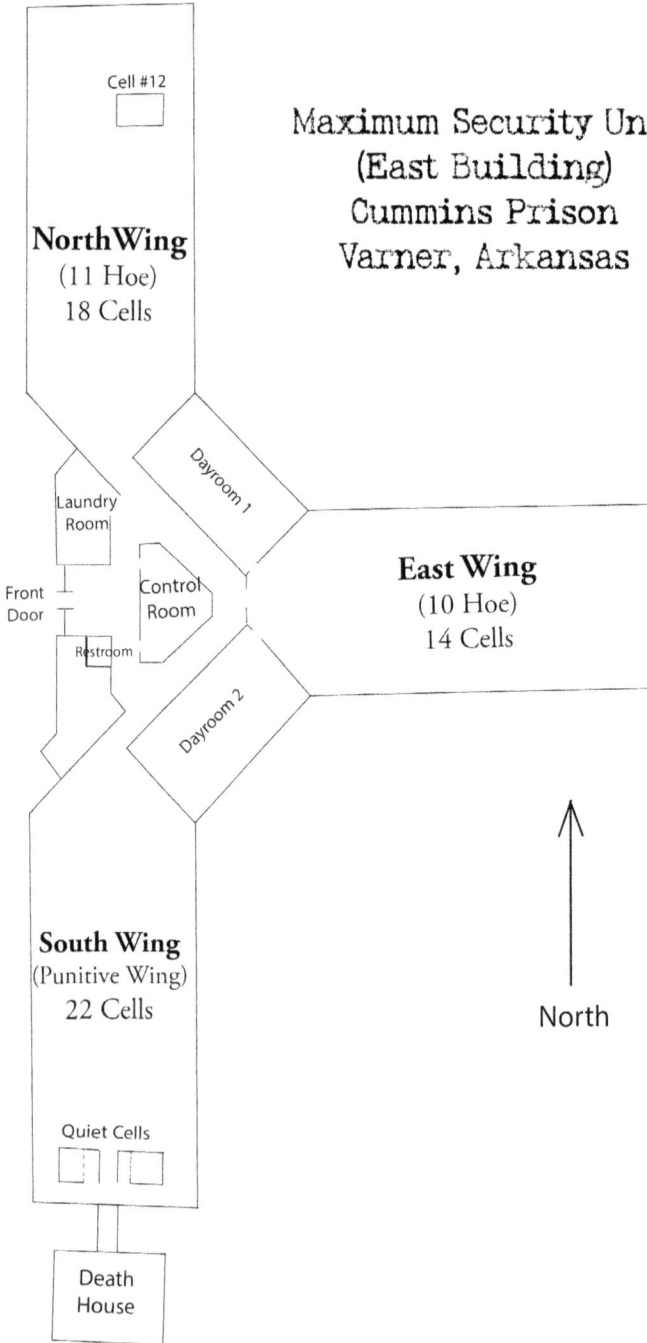

Cell #12

NorthWing
(11 Hoe)
18 Cells

Maximum Security Unit
(East Building)
Cummins Prison
Varner, Arkansas

Dayroom 1

Laundry
Room

Front
Door

Control
Room

East Wing
(10 Hoe)
14 Cells

Restroom

Dayroom 2

South Wing
(Punitive Wing)
22 Cells

North

Quiet Cells

Death
House

Area Map

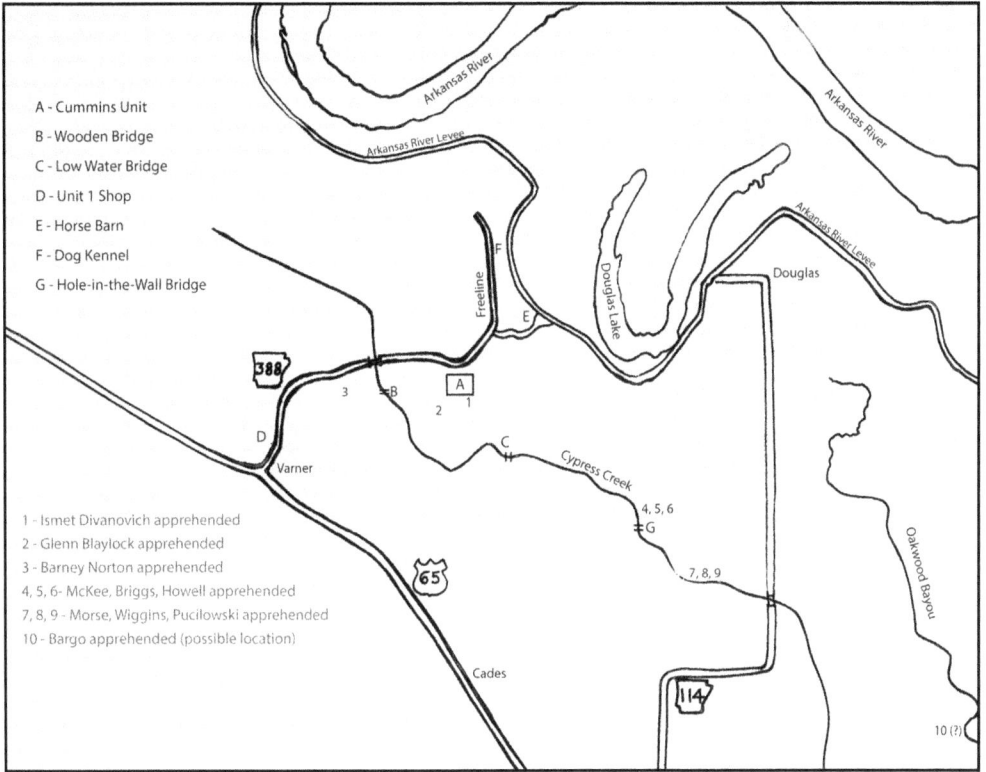

A - Cummins Unit
B - Wooden Bridge
C - Low Water Bridge
D - Unit 1 Shop
E - Horse Barn
F - Dog Kennel
G - Hole-in-the-Wall Bridge

1 - Ismet Divanovich apprehended
2 - Glenn Blaylock apprehended
3 - Barney Norton apprehended
4, 5, 6 - McKee, Briggs, Howell apprehended
7, 8, 9 - Morse, Wiggins, Pucilowski apprehended
10 - Bargo apprehended (possible location)

Arkansas River
Arkansas River Levee
Arkansas River
Arkansas River Levee
Douglas Lake
Douglas
Freeline
388
Varner
65
Cades
114
Cypress Creek
Oakwood Bayou
10 (?)

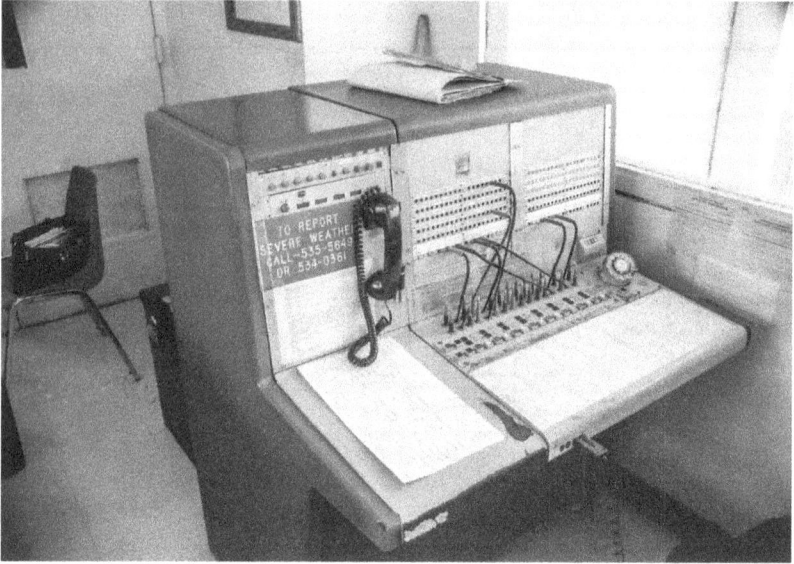

The PBX switchboard

Looking west in the main hall of Cummins. The hall desk can be seen in the distance. The infirmary entrance and pill call window are on the left.

Dayroom 1 as seen from the hallway in the East Building.

East Building Control Room as seen from the lobby.

South Wing of the
East Building, facing
north. Cells are
on the right.

Hall Desk in the main hall of Cummins.

North Wing of the East Building. Notice the stack of mattresses at the end of the hall. Inmates who were assigned to punitive isolation had the mattresses pulled from their cells each morning and did not get them back until the evening.

Paraguard control panel found inside the Armory Tower. The Paraguard system sensed movement by way of pressure on the ground near the fence.

Quiet Cell at the south end of the South Wing of the East Building. The area to the right of the bars was large enough for an officer to be stationed to observe the inmate in the Quiet Cell.

Sally Port Gate on the east side of Cummins. All vehicle traffic entered through this gate. On the night of January 1, it was used as a staging area for officers who were about to enter and take back control of the East Building. The gate is about 600 feet from the East Building.

Sally Port Tower on the east side of Cummins. It was from this tower that the officer first noticed the inmates scaling the fence. In 1979, there was only one fence; the smaller, inner fence. The taller, outer fence was erected not long after the 1979 escapes.

Chapter 17

The Case of Ismet Divanovich

First on the list of complainants was Inmate Ismet Divanovich. He was the escapee who was caught going over the fence on the south side of the compound. After apprehension, he was taken to the front gate by Field Major Dale Reed and Rover Officer Robert Toney. He was turned over to Building Major Billy Taylor and was escorted to Taylor's office for questioning. In the complaint, Divanovich alleges that Taylor struck him on the head with a blackjack. Taylor, in his statement, says that Divanovich was not struck at any time. Divanovich passed a polygraph test when asked if Major Taylor ever struck him with a blackjack. Major Taylor refused to take a polygraph. Infirmary records indicate that Divanovich was examined at approximately 11:00 p.m. and had superficial scratches on his right knee and had a scrape to his right scalp. Neither required stitches and they were painted with "red med," a common term used for merthiolate.

Chapter 18

The Case of Paul Ruiz

Inmate Paul Ruiz's complaint was a little more complex... and interesting. According to a report written by CID Investigator Jack Ursery, Ruiz was in the Control Room of the East Building when the officers were attempting to gain access through the front door. When Ruiz realized the officers were about to gain entrance with a key, he "threw the stick down, punched the electronically controlled buttons to open the doors. He was taken prisoner, handcuffed by Mr. Lockhart, Warden Campbell, and this investigator without incident."

In the report to the Board, "Use of Mace, Gas, or Physical Force by Officers," dated January 1, 1979, the statement reads: "Inmate Ruiz had taken control of the Maximum Security Unit by force along with several other inmates. Inmate Ruiz was in the officers control room along with Inmate Willie Brown, holding two employees hostage with a screwdriver and putty knife. After he was taken prisoner by Lt. E. W. Smith he began struggling and kicking. Lt. Smith struck Inmate Ruiz twice with his slapper. He was then examined by Infirmary Personnel and placed on Punitive Wing."

When other statements are taken into account, the Board report is sketchy and at least to a degree, inaccurate. Ursery's report says that Ruiz was subdued by Lockhart, Campbell, and Ursury. It would be standard practice to handcuff Ruiz while he was lying on the ground face down. After Ruiz was handcuffed, he was apparently placed in the lobby area between the Control Room and the front door of the East Building. He was turned toward the wall where he stood, or possibly knelt, for several hours. He was guarded by Captain A. G. Lucas, Kitchen Supervisor, and Lieutenant E. W. Smith.

Captain Lucas was quite a colorful character. He was not a security officer, but as was stated, was the food service supervisor. He was retired from the Navy. He lived on the freeline. He was known to frequently cuss and was not afraid to get in a verbal altercation with freeworld people and inmates alike. He was also known to enjoy alcohol and, since it was a holiday, had more than likely imbibed in drink during the day and evening leading up to the events of the night of January 1. When he was notified of the disturbance, he came to the unit and entered the building with his own personal .25 caliber revolver. He ended up in the East Building holding said revolver on Inmate Ruiz in the lobby. There are eyewitness accounts that Lucas may have been swaying a bit as he held the gun to Ruiz's ear, asking Ruiz if he believed he (Lucas) would shoot him. Ruiz apparently answered in the affirmative. Lucas was also heard to ask, as he was holding the gun to Ruiz's head, if Ruiz liked the food that was served at the prison. Apparently, Ruiz answered that he did like the food.

Ruiz alleged at one point that Lt. E. W. Smith was holding a .44 magnum to the back of his head and hit him across the back of the head with it. According to Ruiz, Lucas then stated that if Smith was going to strike Ruiz, he should do it right. Lucas then allegedly struck Ruiz across the back of the head.

Medical records indicate that there were three lacerations on Ruiz's head that required a total of 17 stitches. This apparently conflicts with the Board report which says that Ruiz was hit *two* times with the slapper. After X-rays were taken on January 3, it was determined that the skull and spine were normal with no injuries.

On January 10, Lucas said that he had no occasion to strike Ruiz. He stated that "Ruiz did not resist at any time after he was captured." On January 16, Officer Elvis Brown stated that, "Capt. Taylor attempted to handcuff Inmate Ruiz, he resisted. At this time, he was struck twice by Capt. Taylor with a night stick to handcuff him." Three officer statements gave three different accounts of the same incident.

Inmate Ruiz passed the polygraph when asked if Smith and Lucas struck him in the head. Lucas failed the polygraph when asked if he struck Ruiz. In all fairness, however, it appears that in his report, La Plante did not include the entire report from the polygraph exams. There were apparently many questions asked by the examiner, but only a few questions, responses, and the examiner's determination if the answer was truth or deception, were included in La Plante's report. Smith and Taylor refused to take a polygraph test.

It should also be noted that while polygraph tests are used in investigations, they are not allowed as evidence in court. The polygraph test relies on monitoring blood pressure, heart rate, respiration, and perspiration while a person answers questions. The assumption is that a normal person will undergo some physiological changes when he is lying. It is not an exact science and evidence of truth and deception may rely on several factors, including the proficiency of the examiner. There was a case in 1994 when a CIA employee, Aldrich Ames, was arrested for espionage. Aldrich had been a Russian spy for about a decade, but had passed the routine polygraph tests that were mandated by the CIA. How did he do it? He followed the advice of his

Russian handlers, "Just relax, don't worry, you have nothing to fear." He did and he was able to deceive the polygraph.

The American Polygraph Association estimates the accuracy of the polygraph at around 87%, but some scientists claim a lower accuracy rate of around 75%. Because of the possibility that some people who tell the truth may show deception, and some people who are skilled at lying may show truthfulness on a polygraph, the test should be viewed with skepticism, and it should not be the only evidence relied upon to determine the truth.

Even with the possibility that polygraph tests may not be totally reliable and the prospect that the officers and inmates may have presented their own versions of the story, the evidence points to the likelihood that Ruiz was struck while in the lobby of the East Building while he was handcuffed. For one thing, even the officers gave varying accounts of what happened and who hit Ruiz. Then there is Ursery's report written on January 4, indicating that Ruiz was apprehended in the Control Room "without incident." And of course, there is the physical evidence of three lacerations on the scalp taking a total of 17 stitches to suture. The lacerations were not present until after the officers showed up to take back the East Building.

Chapter 19

The Case of Willie Brown

Inmate Willie Brown was in the Control Room along with Ruiz as officers were about enter the East Building. When they came in, Brown ran down the South Wing with the intention of getting back in his cell. When he found the door to his cell locked, he continued down the hall and hid outside of a quiet cell at the very end of the wing.

Ursery's report written on January 4 indicates that "Brown was taken by officers, handcuffed, moved to the front portion of the building, and placed back in his cell, without incident." There is no mention of physical force being used against Brown in the "Use of Mace, Gas, or Physical Force by Officers" reports that were submitted to the Board later in the month.

On January 9, in an interview conducted by George Brewer, Brown indicated that when he got up after being handcuffed outside the quiet cell, Lockhart struck him with the butt of a gun underneath his chin. He said that it did not cause a laceration, but his tongue bled when he bit it after being struck.

On March 13, Lockhart and the newly appointed warden of Cummins, Ronnie Dobbs, interviewed Inmate Brown in the warden's office at Cummins. It was a 25-minute interview in which

Lockhart felt that it showed that there was a case of mistaken identity on the part of Brown and it was someone else who hit Brown, not Lockhart. However, when La Plante interviewed Brown three days later on March 16, Brown said that he told Lockhart something different from the truth because he was afraid and thought he was being recorded and that Lockhart would retaliate against him if he told the truth about Lockhart being the one who hit him. He went on to reconfirm to La Plante that on the night of January 1, Lockhart hit him under the jaw with the butt of a pistol and then put the gun to Brown's head and said that he would kill him. While Brown said that Lockhart was holding a pistol, the evidence suggests that Lockhart entered the East Building with a shotgun.

Later in the evening, approximately two hours after Brown was taken from the quiet cell area and returned to his cell, Sgt. Shugart and Sgt. Moore went to get Brown from his cell and escorted him to the lobby area. He was still in handcuffs. He claimed that Captain Kenny Taylor and Captain Lucas took him into the restroom in the lobby and that Taylor struck him numerous times with a club. He claimed to have also been hit in the face with a fist. Inmate Barney Norton stated that he was sitting on the floor opposite the bathroom entrance and could see Taylor raising his baton to hit Brown but could not see the actual blows. Jimmy Collard, an inmate medic who worked in the infirmary and was in the East Building assisting Mr. Abbott, said that he did not see anything, but did hear noises emanating from the bathroom that sounded like a blunt object being struck against a body. Mark Brewer, another inmate medic, said that he did not see or hear anything, but at one point went to the bathroom to wet a towel and observed Inmate Brown sitting on the floor bleeding from the head. Inmate Chester Treadwell, another medic, stated that he did not hear any noises from the bathroom, but did see Brown with his head bleeding.

Taylor and Lucas emphatically denied hitting Brown. Taylor said that Brown was one of his snitches and he had called Brown to the lobby to get information about the escape. Taylor indicated that Brown told him some things about the other inmates who were involved in the takeover and escape. Lucas was present and spoke with Brown but denied striking him. Lucas further stated that he did not strike a single inmate that entire evening.

When administered a polygraph, the test indicated that Brown was telling the truth when asked if he was struck by Taylor and Lucas. Taylor refused to take the polygraph. When Lucas answered on the polygraph test that he did not strike Willie Brown, his answer showed deception.

At approximately 11:00 p.m. on the night of January 1, Inmate Brown was treated by Infirmary Director Billy Abbott, who was a registered nurse. Brown received nine stitches to a laceration on his scalp and four stitches to his nose. X-rays were taken on January 3 and there were no fractures or dislocations. The evidence indicates that Brown was struck at least twice, and possibly more, on the night of January 1.

Chapter 20

The Case of Glenn Blaylock

Inmate Glenn Blaylock was one of the first inmates returned to the East Building after the escape. He remained on the run for short time before Lt. Floyd McHan apprehended him and brought him back to the compound. Only Divonavich, who was apprehended going over the fence, beat Blaylock back to the building. Blaylock said he was escorted to the East Building by Lt. Jesse Tillar. He stated as he was about to reach the front door of the East Building, Tillar threw him against a pillar just outside the building.

Blaylock said that as he entered the East Building, he was given an order to get down on his knees and face the wall beside Paul Ruiz. He then alleged that he was hit, kicked, and stepped on by several employees, including Capt. Taylor, Capt. Lucas, Officer Brown, A. L. Lockhart, and two unidentified officers. Probably the most egregious allegation was toward Lockhart. Blaylock said that Lockhart stepped on the outside of his right ankle with all his weight and ground it as one would grind out a cigarette.

Taylor stated in an interview with La Plante on January 10 that no one hit Blaylock while he was in the lobby of the East Building. Warden Jerry Campbell also said that he was with Lockhart the entire time and did not see him strike Blaylock "in any fashion whatsoever." There is no mention of force being used against Blaylock in the "Use of Mace, Gas, or Physical Force by Officers" reports that were submitted to the Board later in January.

During a second interview with Lockhart on January 11, he admitted to La Plante that he may have kicked Blaylock, but it was because he had given Blaylock an order to stand up and Blaylock was not complying. He stated that he could have kicked Blaylock one to three times on the feet, shin, or butt. However, he emphatically denied standing on Blaylock's ankle.

Lockhart agreed to a polygraph test and was tested by Robert Blankenship, a private, certified polygraph examiner. The most interesting part of the polygraph test was not the test itself, but the conversation between Blankenship and Lockhart before and after the test. As with La Plante, Lockhart reiterated that he kicked Blaylock but did not step on his ankle. After the test, Lockhart told Blankenship that he did not slap Blaylock, but did turn his head around with his hand. He went on to say that "if he needed to say that he slapped him, on the polygraph, then he slapped him because he has slapped so many prisoners before." From the context, it seems that Lockhart was saying that if he needed to say that he slapped Blaylock during the test for the test to indicate truthfulness, then he would say it. During the test, Lockhart replied "yes" when asked if he slapped Blaylock and the polygraph indicated that Lockhart was truthful.

At the request of Board of Corrections Chairman Richard Earl Griffin, Lockhart was permitted to take a second polygraph test administered by a different examiner. George Stewart of Jonesboro was chosen as the examiner. Only two of an unknown number of questions were listed in La Plante's report, Questions 6 and 7. Question 6 asked if Lockhart intentionally stepped on Blaylock's ankle on January 1. Lockhart answered "no" and his answer indicated truthfulness. Question 7 asked if Lockhart slapped Blaylock on January 1. He answered "yes," and this indicated truthfulness.

There were polygraph tests administered to other employees, but quite frankly, the indications of truthfulness and deception were all over the map. As mentioned earlier, La Plante only chose certain questions and answers that were to be included in the report. Perhaps if all the test results had been included, a clearer picture could be formed.

When Blaylock was examined by medical personnel at approximately 11:00 p.m. on January 1, he was found to have an abrasion to the left ankle and left great toe, an abrasion to the left shoulder and upper arm posterior side. There was also an abrasion to the scalp. There were no sutures required.

Chapter 21

The Case of Barney Norton

Inmate Barney Norton was the third person apprehended following the capture of Divanovich and Blaylock. He was brought back to the East Building through the Sally Port Gate by Red Shadwick and Coleman Knight. As Norton entered the East Building, he was wearing an officer's uniform, a green field jacket, and was layered with clothing underneath. He was soaking wet and no doubt very cold. His hands were secured behind his back with a pair of "flex-cuffs," which are similar to zip ties and are commonly used out in the field. Officers usually did not carry more than one pair of handcuffs and were hesitant to put them on someone who was going to be turned over to someone else, thus increasing the chances that the handcuffs would not be returned.

Norton was one of the ringleaders of the takeover and escape. He had also dealt much misery to prison administration since his arrival to prison in 1975. He was currently in maximum security because he and Earl Van Denton had escaped several months earlier in September.

If there was an eye in the perfect storm, it was the confrontation between Taylor and Norton. Captain Kenny Taylor was the supervisor of the East Building. He was a tough, up-and-coming star in the Department. He had been chosen by the Department to receive special training from the FBI as well as the Arkansas State Police. He had reached the rank of captain and was likely to go further. He had just witnessed the place that he supervised being ransacked and taken over by inmates. He had seen one of his officers taken to the infirmary with a severe cut on his head. A number of inmates had escaped who were under his supervision and violated the security of the Maximum Security Building and Cummins Prison. And who walks in the door in one of his officer's uniforms? The main perpetrator of the whole event. Not only that but Norton had been dealing Taylor misery for some time. Norton complained about everything and admitted nothing. Lucas probably summed up the situation best when he said, "Taylor was pretty shook up," (as Norton entered the East Building after being caught), and "Barney was always bitching about food and everything else."

In the "Use of Mace, Gas, or Physical Force by Officers" that was submitted to the Board later in January, the report read: "Inmate Barney Norton was brought back off of escape and was escorted into the front lobby of the East Building. He was about to be searched when he broke out of a pair of flex cuffs (plastic handcuffs) and lunged at Captain Taylor. Taylor then struck Inmate Norton to subdue him with a night stick. He was treated by Infirmary Personnel and placed in Punitive Isolation." There is no mention of how many times he was struck nor is there mention of a night stick being broken during the encounter.

La Plante's investigation of the Norton incident covers 14 pages and is the classic "he said/she said" between the inmates and the officers. If one is to believe the inmates' statements, then the scenario would go something like this:

> Norton was brought into the East Building and Captain Taylor immediately began hitting Norton in the head with a night stick. Norton wriggled his hands out of the flex cuffs to hold

them up to protect himself. Taylor continued hitting Norton on the head while yelling statements like, "Die, you son-of-a-bitch, die!" and "I'm going to kill you, you stinkin son-of-a-bitch." He also told Norton, "It's payback time, Barney, payback time. Tonight's payback time for all the misery you've caused me." Taylor continued hitting Norton on the head until he broke the night stick. He obtained another one and continued striking Norton for what seemed like 15 minutes. One of the early blows broke Norton's glasses and Lucas picked them up and started poking Norton in the eye with the extended part that goes over the ear.

If one is to believe the officers' statements, then the scenario would go something like this:

When Norton was returned to the East Building, Captain Taylor began shaking him down for contraband. Norton kept turning back and forth as if he were hiding something in his coat pocket that he did not want Taylor to find. Norton then broke out of his flex cuffs and grabbed Taylor around the waist in a bear hug. Taylor struck Norton several times in an attempt to subdue him. During the altercation, Taylor's baton broke, probably due to an air bubble being in the end, making it weaker. During the altercation, Norton kept saying that he had 40 years to do, and he would run every chance he got and would hurt someone if they tried to stop him. Lucas admitted to being present during the altercation, but he was busy guarding Ruiz and didn't see a lot of what was going on. He said he was handed Norton's glasses but did not poke him with them.

All the witnesses, except for Taylor, were given a polygraph test. The tests tended to show that the inmates were truthful in their accounts while the officers were deceptive. However, there were two witnesses who were not officers who witnessed the altercation. David Vidrine and Robert Roden were maintenance workers at Cummins. They were in the building repairing cameras that had been destroyed during the melee. According to Roden, Taylor did not strike Norton until he came out of his flex cuffs, at which time Taylor hit him five or six times. He heard Taylor cussing and calling Norton a son-of-a-bitch.

Vidrine said that Norton was cuffed and was resisting the search. He stated that Taylor hit Norton a couple of times before Norton broke out of the cuffs and threw his hands up. Norton was then hit three or four additional times before being handcuffed again. While Vidrine did not witness the club break as Taylor hit Norton, he did see a broken club lying in the Control Room.

What is the truth about what happened between Taylor and Norton? One will never know, but there are some conclusions that can be drawn from the incident and events leading up to the fateful night. For one thing, Norton had been a rebellious, unruly inmate prior to the event. He engaged in activities that disrupted the order of the institution. He had a previous escape and indicated that he would do it again if given the chance. He never admitted to wrong-doing but was skilled at pointing the finger at authorities.

Taylor, on the other hand, had been violated. His East Building had been trashed by some inmates who had been thorns in the sides of officers and administration. His officers had been overrun and one of them badly hurt in the process. Taylor was livid. He was frustrated. Someone needed to pay. And then Barney Norton walks in wearing the uniform of one of Taylor's officers.

After the altercation, Norton was examined and treated by Billy Abbott, the infirmary administrator. Norton had four separate lacerations to his head. Abbott applied six sutures to a cut above Norton's left eye and 17 sutures to three separate lacerations on the top of his head. There was a superficial laceration to his left wrist and elbow that did not require sutures. There was also a bruise above his left eye. Norton complained of his right ear hurting and when examined later by Dr. Adams, it was found that the eardrum had been perforated. It is clear that Norton received a thorough "head thumping" at the hands of Captain Taylor, with the possibility that others were also involved.

Chapter 22

The Case of Larry Jones and Curtis Austin

Inmates Larry Jones and Curtis Austin alleged they were beaten in Dayroom 1 by several officers, including Capt. Taylor, Officer Elvis Brown, Officer Ronald Moon, Sgt. Pennington, Capt. Lucas, Lt. Gaylon Lay, Sgt. Lloyd Roberts, Lt. Jesse Tillar, Lt. E. W. Smith, Opie McPherson, Officer Michael Holmes, and Sgt. Shugart. Jones and Austin alleged that there were about 10 inmates in Dayroom 1 and all were removed except for Jones and Austin. After all the other inmates left the dayroom, Capt. Taylor turned to all the other officers and stated, "They're all yours." Both inmates insisted that they offered no resistance and after the beating, they were left on the dayroom floor all night.

The officers tell another story. Taylor, Brown, Holmes, and Moon indicated that they were attempting to clear the dayroom and get inmates back to their cells. All the inmates except Jones and Austin complied. All the interviewed officers said that Inmates Jones and Austin backed up against the wall and balled up their fists. The officers then used force to make the inmates comply. Officer Moon stated that Jones began to physically swing at Moon and Taylor. Moon hit Jones with his fist and sustained a broken hand from the encounter. Eventually Jones and Austin were subdued, and medical personnel were summoned to tend to the wounds.

The "Use of Mace, Gas, or Physical Force by Officers" report that was submitted to the Board later in January contained information that was consistent with the statements made by the officers. The report read, "Inmate Larry Jones and Curtis Austin were in dayroom one after escaping off of Punitive Wings. They were ordered out of the dayroom and did not move. They were ordered a second time to come out and they still ignored the orders. Captain Taylor, East Building Supervisor then ordered the officers present to enter the dayroom and remove the two inmates. Inmates Jones and Austin then backed up against the wall and doubled up their fists. When the officers approached Jones and Austin, the inmates attacked. Officers Brown, Moon, Stewart and others struck the two inmates several times with slappers and night sticks before the inmates were subdued. The infirmary was called and the inmates refused medical treatment and were placed on Punitive. Later the next day they did allow the Infirmary Personnel to treat them."

Jones was examined and had six stitches placed in his left hand and three in his lower left leg. He had abrasions to his scalp but required no stitches. An X-ray revealed that Jones had a fracture in his left forearm. His arm would later be put in a cast. Austin had a laceration in his scalp that needed sutures, but he refused all medical treatment. On January 9, Austin still refused medical treatment, but his leg was X-rayed, and it was determined that he had a fracture in his left fibula. He was placed on six-week bedrest and instructed to walk with crutches and not put any weight on that leg until it healed. He was isolated in the infirmary during the six-week recovery time.

This is an incident that tends to point to the officers' stories being correct. All the officers who gave statements were consistent in their description of events. When Jones was given a polygraph, the results indicated he was deceptive on all the questions that bolstered his side of the story. There is no record of Austin taking the polygraph.

Chalk one up for the officers.

Chapter 23

The Case of Ronney Briggs, Terry Howell, and Jerry McKee

Inmates Ronney Briggs, Terry Howell, and Jerry McKee were the fourth, fifth, and sixth escapees apprehended at approximately 4:30 a.m. on January 2 by Van Myers and Lt. Jimmy Dougan. Warden Jerry Campbell and CID Investigator Jack Ursery drove them back to Cummins after the apprehension.

Briggs, Howell, and McKee were three of the inmates who had taken the "vow of the Nazarite" and were wearing long hair and beards. They had filed a lawsuit in federal court saying that they should be allowed to grow long hair and beards because of a sincerely held religious belief. The case was not scheduled to go before the judge until sometime in February, but until then, the inmates were refusing to conform to the grooming policy formulated by the Department. The court would eventually rule in the inmates' favor and the Department would have to allow inmates who took the vow of the Nazarite an exception to the grooming policy.

After receiving a haircut and shave and having their photographs taken in the photo lab, the three inmates were returned to the East Building. The three allege that as they entered the

East Building they were handcuffed and ordered to line up against the wall in the lobby, the same wall where Ruiz and Blaylock had been standing, or kneeling, earlier in the evening. They stated that they were then beaten with nightsticks and kicked by Capt. Taylor, Lt. Lay, Sgt. Roberts, Lt. Tillar, Sgt. Pennington, and other officers.

While the inmates focused on the beatings, the officers' statements added context as to why physical force was used on the inmates. The officers indicated that when the three inmates were returned to the East Building, they were using derogatory language toward staff and complaining about getting their hair cut. Taylor stated that the inmates were uncuffed so that they could be searched. When Taylor reached toward Briggs to search him, Briggs pushed his hand away. Taylor then struck Briggs with a nightstick. As soon as Taylor struck Briggs, Howell and McKee attacked Taylor. At that point, Taylor said "We just started fighting." Lay, Roberts, Tillar and Pennington joined in the fracas and according to Lay, the inmates were struck "until they stopped struggling."

In the "Use of Mace, Gas, or Physical Force by Officers" report that was submitted to the Board later in January the following account of the incident is given, "Inmates Terry Howell, ADC# 67967, Jerry McKee, ADC# 70856, and Ronnie Briggs, ADC# 64584, were escorted back to the East Building. While they were in the lobby of the East Building they were cursing and using derogatory language, they were ordered to stop. When Captain Taylor went to search Inmate Briggs, he slapped Captain Taylor's hand away. At this time Inmate Briggs was struck by Captain Taylor with a night stick. Inmate Howell and McKee started towards Captain Taylor to assist Inmate Briggs. Lt. Lay, Sgt. Roberts, Sgt. Pennington, and Lt. Tillar helped to subdue all three inmates. Inmates Briggs, Howell, and McKee were struck several times with slappers and night sticks. They were then treated by Infirmary Personnel and placed on Punitive Wing of the East Building." There is nothing in the report that indicates whether the inmates were handcuffed during the incident.

The infirmary was called after the encounter, and personnel came to the East Building to provide medical attention. According to the medical documents, there were two entries made about each of these inmates that morning. The first entry was made not long after they were returned to the compound after their escape, before they were returned to the East Building. The second entry cataloged their injuries after they had been returned to the East Building and had an encounter with Taylor and the other officers.

Briggs was examined at approximately 5:30 a.m. when he was first returned to the compound. At that time, it was noted that he had two small scratches to the back of his neck and a small cut on his index finger. His physical condition was noted to be good. The next entry at approximately 7:00 a.m., indicated that Briggs had three lacerations on his head which required 28 stitches and two lacerations on his lower leg which required nine stitches.

When Jerry McKee was first returned to the compound, medical records indicated that he had scratches to the right inside of his knee, scratches and abrasions on both legs, and a small blister on his right heel. No stitches were required, and merthiolate was applied after the wounds were cleaned. The next medical entry at approximately 7:00 a.m. indicated that McKee had a laceration on his head that required seven stitches and a bruise on his lower lip.

When Terry Howell was returned to the compound, medical records indicate that he had one small abrasion on the inside of his right knee. His general condition was noted as good. The next entry at approximately 7:00 a.m. indicates that Howell had contusions and bruises on his head and shoulders. No stitches were required.

There is one additional twist to this incident. During La Plante's investigation, an "Officer Doe" came forward with a statement about the beatings. Officer Doe (pseudonym) was present during the incident and wrote a witness statement that supported the other reports made by the officers at the time. However, on February 14, Officer Doe told La Plante that Briggs, Howell, and McKee were handcuffed in the lobby when they were struck by officers. He also indicated that Lt. Tillar kicked one of the inmates so hard that he split the front of one of his shoes.

Briggs was the only inmate who eventually took a polygraph test regarding the incident. The answers that Briggs gave indicated that he was telling the truth when he stated that he was handcuffed when Taylor and Roberts hit him with a baton and slapper. Officer Doe also took a polygraph test and it indicated that he was being truthful when he stated that Briggs was handcuffed when he was hit by Taylor. None of the other officers or inmates took a polygraph test.

Chapter 24

The Case of Johnny Wiggins

Inmate Johnny Wiggins, along with Ronnie Pucilowski and Gary Morse, was apprehended at approximately 8:30 a.m. about a half mile southeast of the Hole-in-the-Wall Bridge beside Nineteen Canal. They were the seventh, eighth, and ninth escapees caught. Pucilowski and Morse had lost their shoes and were suffering from frostbite, so they were taken directly to the infirmary and eventually to the hospital in Pine Bluff. Wiggins was not so lucky. Wiggins, who was the porter who rushed Officer Bryant at the beginning of the takeover, was now back in the East Building facing Bryant's supervisor, Capt. Kenny Taylor.

All the officers' statements indicated that when Wiggins was returned to the East Building, he was searched and returned to his cell without incident. Wiggins and "Officer Doe" tell a somewhat different version of the story. Wiggins claimed that upon return to the East Building, Taylor pushed him into the restroom in the lobby area and beat him. He also stated that he was beaten by other officers while being escorted to his cell on the punitive wing. Officer Doe stated that Wiggins was not handcuffed when he returned to the East Building. He further stated that Wiggins was taken into the bathroom in the lobby and worked over by

Taylor with a slapper. Upon being escorted to his cell, Officer Doe said that several officers hit Wiggins while he was in the hallway just behind the Control Room.

Wiggins was examined by medical staff before being returned to the East Building. His feet had been soaked in water to warm them up. He had abrasions to both ankles but there were no other bruises or abrasions noted. His abrasions were cleaned, and merthiolate was applied. He was not examined again by medical personnel, but when he was interviewed on January 4, La Plante observed that there was a long reddish welt on Wiggins's back and several small bruises on his chest. When Tim Baltz, at the request of La Plante, went to Cummins on January 5 to photograph the injuries of the various inmates, it was noted by Baltz that no photograph was taken of Wiggins because there was "nothing left to photograph—claimed he had been hit."

Chapter 25

Medical Treatment Protocol

Infirmary Administrator Billy Abbott, a registered nurse, was on call that night. He was notified by the PBX operator to report to the building just as the officers were reporting when the escape happened. Most of the inmates involved in the takeover and escape were not brought to the infirmary; they were taken directly to the East Building. Abbott was notified to bring over medical supplies and treat the inmates in the East Building. He told his inmate medics, Chester Treadwell and Jimmy Collard, to get some medical supplies together and go with him to the East Building. With stethoscopes, bandages, merthiolate, and sutures in tow, they proceeded the short distance down the hall and out the back door to the East Building lobby. When they arrived, Abbott asked for a table to be set up. There was no table. Abbott eventually started having the inmates sit against the wall of the lobby while he and the inmate medics started cleaning wounds, sewing up cuts, and applying "red med," another name for merthiolate. Abbott indicated that he did not see any of the physical force that was going on, only the results of it. He said there was a whole lot of noise—yelling, cussing, and the like, but he was intent on doing his job of sewing up inmates and didn't pay much attention to what was going on around him.

In all the turmoil, Abbott related one humorous story. As he worked his way down the wall lined with injured inmates, he came upon one inmate who was covered in blood. As the inmate medics began to clean him up, they discovered that he had no cuts or abrasions, only blood. The inmate explained that he was sitting between two other inmates who received beatings and their blood got on him. When officers got to him, they assumed that he already had his "head thumping" and moved on. The inmate pleaded with Abbott to put some stitches in his head. Abbott told him that he didn't have any cuts to stitch up. After additional pleading, Abbott had the inmate medic shave a place on the inmate's head. Abbott made a small incision at the spot and then added six to seven sutures, thus assuring that the inmate would not be bothered any more with the possibility of a head thumping, since it was evident he had already gotten one.

While Wiggins was sent to the East Building, Pucilowski and Morse remained in the infirmary due to the severe frostbite in their lower extremities. Abbott related that it wasn't long before a "goon squad" showed up in the infirmary from the East Building with the intention of giving Pucilowski and Morse their just punishment for running off. Abbott told the officers that if they assaulted the two inmates, they would have to take him on as well. The officers indicated that they could easily do that, but Abbott further explained that when he testified in federal court, he would relate the truth about the whole incident. After some additional exchange about snitching and such, the officers left without further thought of physical assault. Since Pucilowski and Morse were transferred to the hospital shortly after and never received the head thumping they were due.

Chapter 26

Events After the Event

Much of the early discussion in the days after the escapes centered on how to prevent inmates from escaping. Policies at the time were vague. If an officer sees an inmate headed toward the fence, what does he do? Yell, "Halt"? Fire a warning shot? Shoot to maim? Shoot to kill? How far away from the fence does an inmate have to be before he is fired on? Does he have to be on the fence or just getting close to the fence?

To muddle the discussion even further, there was an escape at Cummins two years prior to the January 1 escape when two inmates scaled the fence and were shot by prison personnel. One inmate was killed and the other seriously wounded. In the aftermath, the warden resigned and moved out of state and several high-ranking officials and officers were fired. The general discussion among the ranks was that they were fired because they used deadly force on escaping inmates. This was not the case, however. They were fired for falsifying reports surrounding the escape, but the myth of using deadly force on fleeing inmates as the cause of the firings still thrived. In a reference to this, Lockhart commented that officers failed to shoot on the night of January 1 because they feared losing their jobs or possible suits brought against them in federal court. He noted that 11 shots were fired at the fleeing inmates, and not one was hit. He was quoted in the *Arkansas Gazette* as saying, "They didn't want to hit them."

These questions and concerns were discussed by Board Chairman Richard Earl Griffin in a press conference on January 4, 1979. He vowed that the Board would adopt a policy at their meeting later in the month outlining what officers should do when faced with a fleeing inmate. The tenor of Griffin's remarks indicated that the Board was fully in favor of using whatever force necessary to stop escaping inmates. He gave assurance that the Board would stand behind any officer who used force, even deadly force, in the line of duty. He also indicated that if officers would not use the necessary force to stop fleeing inmates, they would be replaced by officers who would. Griffin's remarks were emphatic.

At the Board meeting on January 25, the policy discussion on use of force may not have been the most interesting discussion at the meeting. The most curious dialogue may have been the exchange between board members and three wives of inmates who were there to recommend conjugal visits. After a lengthy discussion the issue was laid to rest and the Board delayed any action that might satisfy the wives…and their incarcerated husbands. They then turned their attention to the adoption of the Use of Force policy proposed by Director Mabry.

The Board not only had the proposed policy but also an opinion from the Attorney General regarding the use of force. It was Attorney General Steve Clark's opinion that three events must occur in the use of deadly force. "First, if the inmate is on or near the fence and appears to be attempting to escape, the officer must verbally warn the inmate to halt. Second, if the inmate ignores the officer's warning, and reaches or is on the fence, then the officer must fire a preliminary warning shot. Third, if thereafter the officer believes the inmate is attempting to escape and that deadly force is necessary to prevent it then the officer may use deadly force to stop the inmate."

Despite the rhetoric of the previous month and a lengthy discussion at the board meeting, the Board eventually decided to delay approving a policy at the request of Director Mabry "until he and the Assistant Directors can meet with Mr. Kirkpatrick (Corrections Coordinator, Office of the Attorney General) and draft an overall policy that will apply to most situations."

Within the next few days, the focus would shift from firing on escaping inmates to the events that happened within the East Building after the escapees were returned. News of La Plante's investigation surfaced in the *Pine Bluff Commercial* on February 2. The headline of the article written by Russell D. Hemphill screamed, "Inmate Beatings Alleged." From that point forward, the attention was not on what the officers did or didn't do as inmates climbed over the fence, but on what officers did or didn't do when inmates were returned to custody.

Chapter 27

What If?

King Solomon, widely recognized as the wisest person who ever lived, said, "The person who tells one side of a story seems right, until someone else comes and asks questions." Proverbs 18:17 (NCV). Stephen La Plante was in the right place at the right time to ask questions about the events of that night.

What if there had been no Stephen La Plante on January 1, 1979? What if he had showed up for work on January 4, 1979, instead of December 4, 1978? What if there had not been a consent decree in which the very first condition was: "No Arkansas Department of Corrections employee will use excessive force against any inmate?" Very likely the public reporting and outcome of the events of January 1-2, 1979, would have been quite different. The Department would have been lauded for quelling a disturbance and capturing all escaped convicts within 24 hours without any citizens getting hurt and no property destroyed. The four "Use of Mace, Gas, or Physical Force by Officers," reports presented in the January board packet would have been accepted without question. After all, these officers were dealing with desperados. They were bad people. They were rapists, thieves, and murderers. So what if the officers had to use physical force to get the inmates to submit to shakedowns or get them to return to their cells? They probably deserved what they got, right?

The problem was one word in the consent decree, "excessive." What is excessive? Can an officer use force to make an inmate submit to a shakedown? Sure. Can an officer use force when an inmate refuses to move where the officer tells him? Sure. Can an officer crack an inmate on the head with a pistol when the inmate is on his knees, facing the wall, handcuffed behind his back? A reasonable person would say that is excessive and uncalled for. Can a squad of officers go into a room and physically beat down inmates who refuse to come out? The courts would probably say that officers can use force, but only the force necessary to get the prisoners to comply, not the kind that causes broken arms and legs.

La Plante's first report to the federal court as compliance coordinator centered on the use of excessive force against 11 inmates on January 1-2, 1979. It was over 100 pages and would touch the conscience of the Department. It would influence future policy and practices of handling inmate misbehavior, evolving from emotional to professional responses by officers.

Chapter 28

Watergate, Arkansas Style

By February 9, La Plante's investigation was well underway. Inmates had been interviewed and most, if not all, had completed their polygraph tests. When Deborah Miller, La Plante's administrative assistant, got to work on Friday, February 9, she discovered what appeared to be a break-in. One of her desk drawers was ajar, the copy machine felt warm to the touch, and the counter on the copy machine registered 150 copies that were unaccounted for. There was, however, no sign of forced entry. La Plante indicated that his files had been rifled through. He speculated that someone who wanted to know the results of the polygraph tests broke in and copied the not-yet-released papers.

La Plante did not report the break-in to police until Saturday, the day after the alleged burglary. The Pine Bluff Police Chief, Bobby Norman, said that the investigation was hampered due to a day of business being conducted before the break-in was reported. Evidence, such as fingerprints, would have been destroyed due to the delay.

While La Plante continued to insist that his office had been burglarized, the police were not so sure. They eventually closed the case on March 7, with no arrests. In Norman's public statement about the matter, he said that the police concluded that the office was never burglarized. They believed that the desk drawer was accidentally left unlocked and the 150 copies on the copy machine could be explained by another office using it the day before the copy machine was moved into La Plante's office. La Plante was still not convinced. In a letter addressed to the three inmate attorneys and Director Mabry on February 27, La Plante stated, "You are all aware of the fact that some person or persons unknown entered my office early in the morning of February 9, ostensibly to make a xerox copy of my notes in this investigation as well as the polygraph results on the inmates." He was quoted in the *Arkansas Gazette* on March 9, as saying, "I do think every effort was made by the burglar or burglars to make it appear as if nothing had happened." It is clear from his comments that La Plante was never convinced that the break-in did not occur.

Chapter 29

The Writing on the Wall

Before the days of social media, a popular way to express one's opinion was to send a letter to the local newspaper editor and hopefully have it printed in the opinion section of the paper. An added benefit was that one could ask that the name not be attached to the ending of the letter, in which case the letter would end with "Name Withheld."

In the days and weeks following the incident, there was a steady stream of letters submitted to and printed in the *Pine Bluff Commercial*. Only two days after the news article was published about an ongoing investigation, the wife of a Cummins officer wrote a letter that was printed in the *Commercial*. She expressed weariness from all the convicts crying about mistreatment. She went on to show support for the underpaid, overworked employees who were dedicated and hard-working. In the letter, she encouraged the Governor to stand behind the officers and the administration of the Department.

Not surprisingly, almost all the letters from the public were in support of the prison guards and the administration. Also, not surprisingly, almost all the letters were signed "Name Withheld." One letter asked what should be done in such a circumstance.

"What should the guards say, 'Now, Now boys, let's get back in our cells and be good boys.' Needless to say it would much (sic) easier for employees to let them have an easy escape and let them run wild through the streets to terrorize those they missed on their first spree." Another "Name Withheld" opined, "They (prisoners) are sent to prison to serve their time for whatever crime they may have committed, not to incite riots within the prison, not to plot to escape at no matter what cost or whose life they may take."

One "Name Withheld" letter was purportedly written by an officer who worked at Cummins. In it, he commended the actions of his fellow officers and assailed the conduct of the prisoners. He wrote, "I am about to pop open with disgust. Disgust with the news media, Mr. La Plante, Mr. Kaplan and the federal judges. In the first place, what all of you seemed to forget is none of the inmates at Cummins Prison are there for going to Church on Sunday and saying their Sunday School lesson. So why take their side and believe them. They are there (or here) for committing a crime. Some of them are horrible crimes. Crimes they could have committed against your family and friends." These thoughts are indicative of most of the public at the time. The general thought was that these were bad people and deserving of whatever punishment they got while in prison.

One of the few opposing letters was written by Barney Norton, the mastermind of the insurrection by the inmates. In a letter published in the *Pine Bluff Commercial* on April 3, 1979, Norton opined, "We have a number of sadistic officers who quite literally believe they are here to punish the inmates by acts of brutality, representative of a demented mind not equipped to sustain the psychological and emotional pressure caused by the job." He went on to say, "They fell (sic) to understand what Judge Eisele ment (sic) when he said we are here 'as punishment' and not 'for punishment'. The Arkansas Department of Correction is a fine example of what Chief Justice Burger ment (sic) when he said, 'we have developed systems of corrections which do not correct.'"

From these letters one can see the divergent opinions depending on which side of the fence one resides. In looking back years after the event, journalist Bill Sadler commented that the residents of Southeast Arkansas at the time really didn't care if an inmate got his head thumped. The officers and administration had broad public support while the inmates had only a handful of lawyers, and some would say La Plante, looking out for their interests.

Chapter 30

The Board

In 1979, the Arkansas Board of Corrections was composed of five regular members and an ex-officio law enforcement member, all appointed by the governor. Richard Earl Griffin, an attorney from Crossett, was serving as chair. Eula Dorsey, from West Memphis, was serving as vice-chair. Other members included Dr. Thomas Wortham, a physician from Jacksonville; John Elrod, an attorney from Siloam Springs; Bill Bevis, a farmer from Scott; and Jim Rhodes, an attorney from DeValls Bluff.

During the early months of 1979, the Board found itself in a very difficult situation. An end to oversight by the federal court was within reach. A consent decree had been signed. All the Department had to do was honor the orders of the court, including the 39 articles of the consent decree. And then a bunch of inmates decided to take over the East Building and wreak havoc during a 15-hour escape. If that were not enough, officers added to the complications by using force on inmates as they were returned to the East Building. Things were a mess. The Board needed to act cautiously lest they alienate the federal courts on one side and give the indication of not supporting staff and administration on the other.

Adding to the confusion, Director James Mabry turned in his resignation on March 1, effective June 1. The resignation was prompted by discussion during the executive session of the February 28 Board meeting. From all indications the Board and Mabry had experienced a tenuous relationship for some time, and the current events exacerbated the relationship. Board Chairman Richard Earl Griffin said that Mabry's decision to resign was a "mutual decision" between the Board and Mabry. Griffin expressed that there were "some people on the board not pleased with his progress or that of the department." In his resignation letter, Mabry expressed his frustration by saying that he was sure that the person the Board wanted as director did not exist.

With Mabry on his way out, the leadership of the Department essentially fell to Assistant Director Art Lockhart. This added to the complications, since Lockhart was one of the individuals accused of excessive force in La Plante's report. This dilemma was expressed in a March 9 article in the *Arkansas Democrat*. Reporter James Taylor wrote, "News accounts from the week of the escape quote prison officials as saying that A. L. "Art" Lockhart, assistant commissioner of institutional services, was heading the department's internal investigation of the escape. The *Democrat* source has said that information gathered by La Plante has identified Lockhart as a participant in activities that led to the inmate allegations." While the Board only had the four physical force reports that were prepared by the Department available to them at the February 28 meeting, it is clear that elements of La Plante's investigation were beginning to leak out to the press.

By Wednesday, March 28, La Plante's report was complete with a copy delivered to Board Chairman Richard Earl Griffin, Director Jim Mabry, and the attorneys for the inmates. After reading the report, Griffin commented, "there are certainly indications that excessive force was used." In responding to Griffin's remarks, Phillip Kaplan, one of the attorneys for the inmates, commented, "I'd say his statement was temperate in view of what's in the report." It was clear that the bombshell was about to drop.

In addition to the investigation report, La Plante compiled a separate report in which he scored the level of proof regarding each accusation of excessive physical force. The levels ranged from "Preponderance," wherein a majority of the evidence supports a finding to "Clear and Convincing," wherein at least three-fourths of the evidence supports the finding. In addition, he recommended several categories of dispositions, which included sustained, exonerated, inconclusive, and unfounded.

Chapter 31

The Findings of the Board

The Board convened at 3:10 p.m. on March 30 at the Pine Bluff Central Office. After discussing some regular business, Chairman Griffin entertained a motion for the Board to "convene in executive session for the purpose of considering the Compliance Coordinator's report and any personnel and/or disciplinary matters that may result from the report." The Board went into executive session at 4:20 p.m. and did not reconvene in regular session until 7:15 p.m.

Upon emerging from the executive session, Griffin recapped the injuries the inmates received that night. He said, "There is some conflict as to how the cuts occurred, but it was as a result of confrontations with officers." This statement seems to indicate that the Board, or at least Griffin, felt that the officers were at least partially provoked into action by the inmates.

Griffin went on to say, "there is no doubt, and I want to make it clear, that these injuries were received because of force. The question, of course, that the Board has to determine is whether or not that force was excessive in accordance with the policies of the Department of Corrections and, of course, the prior orders of the Federal Court, and if the force was excessive, what disciplinary actions to take, if any."

Griffin then entertained a motion to recommend disciplinary action against the officers who refused to take the polygraph test. The recommendation was that "in each instance where an employee received a direct command to take the polygraph examination, and in the face of that, refused to do so, that employee receive a letter of reprimand in his personnel file and be placed on six months (sic) probation." The motion was passed with only one "no" vote by Bevis, who stated that he supported the reprimand, but not the six months' probation. According to La Plante's investigation report, the following officers were requested to take the polygraph and refused: Major B. G. Taylor, Captain Kenny Taylor, Lt. E. W. Smith, Lt. L. M. Smith, Lt. Jesse Tillar, Lt. Gaylon Lay, and Sgt. Lloyd Roberts.

The next motion that Griffin entertained dealt with allegations of excessive force by Sgt. Lloyd Roberts and Lt. Gaylon Lay. Both officers were mentioned in two altercations the night of January 1. The first was the altercation in which Inmates Jones and Austin were physically removed from Dayroom 1. La Plante had determined that the evidence was inconclusive whether excessive force had been used. The other was the Briggs/Howell/McKee altercation in which a fight broke out between the inmates and the officers. La Plante determined that the evidence was clear and convincing that excessive physical force had been used. The Board was unanimous in recommending that the two receive a letter of reprimand and be reduced one step in pay for their use of excessive physical force.

Chairman Griffin then entertained a motion to reduce Lt. Jesse Tillar to sergeant and place him on six months' probation for use of excessive force. The motion passed unanimously. Tillar was mentioned in the Blaylock incident, the Jones/Austin altercation in the dayroom, and the Briggs/Howell/McKee clash. In the Briggs/Howell/McKee incident, La Plante reported that the complaint was sustained against Tillar based on clear and convincing evidence.

Next, Chairman Griffin entertained a motion that Lt. E. W. Smith be reduced to sergeant and be placed on one year probation for his part in using excessive force. The motion passed unanimously. Smith is mentioned in La Plante's report in the Ruiz incident, when Smith allegedly hit Ruiz in the head with the butt of his revolver. He is also mentioned in the Jones/Austin incident in Dayroom 1. In the Ruiz incident, La Plante determined that the use of excessive force was sustained by clear and convincing evidence. La Plante went on to say that in the Ruiz incident, "Lieutenant Smith claimed he struck because of some resistance. There was no resistance."

Before the Board recessed at 7:35 p.m., they had meted out discipline for seven employees for failing to take the polygraph test and four employees for using excessive force. The next day, during questions and answers with media representatives, Chairman Griffin indicated that the Board believed that the four who were disciplined were not criminally wrong in what they did.

The actions of the Board were closely watched by the attorneys for the inmates. Several days after the board meeting, Philip Kaplan vowed to release the La Plante report to the public. Up to this time, the report remained undisclosed to everyone except the Board of Corrections, the ADC Commissioner, and the attorneys for the inmates. Kaplan expressed displeasure with the Board for not taking stronger action against employees who were accused of using excessive force.

Kaplan made the investigation public on April 4. He is quoted in the *Arkansas Gazette* as saying, "The public deserves and needs to know that they're not in compliance with the decree." Kaplan went on to say that he was going to ask Judge Eisele to review the report and hold the Corrections Board in contempt of court.

What seemed to upset Kaplan the most was that the Board had appointed Lockhart to be Operational Manager of the Department, which effectively made him interim director. It seemed to Kaplan that the Board was rewarding Lockhart while at the same time he was under suspicion of being one of the employees who was using excessive force on the night of January 1. He was quoted on April 5th in the *Pine Bluff Commercial* as saying, "the Board's action on Lockhart indicated that the Board did not plan to comply with the consent decree."

The Board held a special session on April 7 at the Cummins Unit to discuss the accusations against three employees, A. L. Lockhart, A. G. Lucas, and Captain Kenny Taylor. At the beginning of the meeting Board Member John Elrod commented that since there had originally been 16 accused employees using excessive physical force, and the Board was only hearing the cases of seven. This effectively meant that nine employees had been exonerated by the Board. These included Officer Elvis Brown, Lt. Arthur Hall, Officer Michael Holmes, Sgt. H. King, Opie McPherson, Officer Ronald Moon, Sgt. George Pennington, Sgt. L. O. Shugart, and Major Billy Taylor.

On the evening of April 6, the night before the board meeting, several of the Board members went to Cummins and talked with some of the inmates who were involved in the altercations. This was done in the name of gaining further information by the Board. Elrod was assigned to talk to Inmate Ruiz, but Ruiz refused to talk to him. Bevis spoke with Inmate Willie Brown. Dr. Wortham interviewed Inmate Blaylock. Elrod and Rhodes spoke with Inmate Barney Norton.

The Board entered executive session at 9:30 a.m. on April 7. Lockhart was interviewed 9:40–10:35. Taylor talked with the Board 10:35 – 11:08. Lucas was in with the Board 11:15 – 11:25. Jack Ursery was interviewed by the Board beginning at 11:25, but a few minutes after Ursery entered the executive session, Reporter Victoria Hirschland from the *Pine Bluff Commercial* interrupted the executive session complaining that since Ursery was not an employee of the Department, it was a violation of the Freedom of Information Act (FOI) for the Board to meet privately with him. Neal Kirkpatrick from the Attorney General's office opined that it was probably not a violation of the FOI since Ursery was detailed and assigned to the Department of Corrections, but Chairman Griffin decided not to take any chances and ended the conversation, saying that any further discussion with Ursery would be held in an open forum.

The Board instructed Tim Baltz to ask the four employees who had been previously disciplined if they wanted to meet while the Board was in executive session. Lt. Lay indicated he had nothing else to say; Sgt. Smith was not present; Sgt. Roberts was no longer employed by the Department. However Sgt Tillar did ask to meet with the Board and did so for about 30 minutes.

As the Board reconvened in regular session at 1:10 p.m., the first item on the agenda was the consideration of the actions of A. L. Lockhart. He had been involved in two incidents in the East Building, the Willie Brown altercation, and the Glen Blaylock incident. In the Willie Brown incident in which Lockhart allegedly struck Brown with the butt of his pistol under his chin, La Plante, in his report, listed the complaint that Lockhart had used excessive force as sustained with clear and convincing evidence. In the incident involving Inmate Glen Blaylock, in which Lockhart allegedly kicked Blaylock while he was handcuffed and possibly slapped him, La Plante found that the evidence that Lockhart had used excessive force was sustained with clear and convincing evidence.

Chairman Griffin asked for a motion "concerning whether or not there is a finding of excessive force on the part of Mr. Art Lockhart, Assistant Director of the Department of Correction?"

Board Member John Elrod moved, "that we make a specific finding that no excessive force under the surrounding circumstances was employed by Art Lockhart on the night in question, and that we recommend no disciplinary action whatsoever be taken against him." The motion was seconded by Board Member Eula Dorsey. When the vote was taken, it was unanimous.

After the vote, Chairman Griffin gave a lengthy explanation as to why the Board concluded what it did. He said, "We took into consideration all the circumstances and these allegations were made at a time within a 10 or 15, maybe a 30-minute period that ... control of the building was being taken by Mr. Lockhart. There were approximately 90 inmates loose in the building at that time. He was unaware whether or not they were armed. He was unaware as to where four hostages were that were in the building. We had one employee who had been injured, lying on the floor in his blood. There were certainly unusual circumstances, and we feel like that to take over the control of the building under those conditions with no more injury than occurred at that time was appropriate, and we want to commend Mr. Lockhart for no more, no one suffering anymore injury up until that time than was suffered. The other incidents involve later conduct. The situation changed. We had assumed control of the building. We were aware of how many inmates were out. We began to become aware that the inmates were unarmed. The hostages had been released. We had assumed control of the building, and we feel at that time that circumstances changed, as they changed throughout the night."

Griffin transitioned to the consideration of the Taylor incidents by saying, "The next incident occurred later with Captain Kenny Taylor and the Barney Norton incident, which is incident number six in the Compliance Coordinator's report. This incident occurred after Mr. Barney Norton had been returned to the East

Building after leaving the building. The Barney Norton incident with Captain Taylor and then the Ruiz incident with Captain Taylor and then the Willie Brown incident involving allegations involving Captain Taylor, and these allegations and these events occurred at a different time."

In the Ruiz case, La Plante had ruled the evidence was inconclusive as to whether Taylor used excessive force, but in the Norton and Brown cases, La Plante said that the complaints were sustained by clear and convincing evidence that excessive physical force had been used by Taylor.

When Griffin called for a motion, Dr. Wortham moved that Taylor be found guilty of excessive force. It was seconded by Elrod and passed unanimously. After the vote determining the force was excessive, the Board then had to make a recommendation on discipline to be imposed. Again, Griffin gave a lengthy discourse before asking for a motion on recommended discipline. He said, "In his defense, it has been called to our attention that he's been an employee with this Department since 1971 or '72. He has received training at the F.B.I. Academy, at the State Police Academy. There's been instances, it's been called to our attention that in Pine Bluff, an armed inmate was held up in a home or under a home in Pine Bluff, and he went to the location at the risk of bodily injury to himself and while under apparent ability and authority to injure the inmate, was successful in talking this inmate out of the building without incident and disarmed the inmate. There are several incidents where Captain Taylor used a great deal of discretion, forethought, and wisdom with the Department. The fact remains though, obvious to this Board, that more force than necessary was used in the January 1-2 incident, and the fact remains that we're under Court order to eliminate excessive force. We have repeatedly made it clear to the staff, and we hope that the employees can understand that excessive force will not, cannot, and shall not be tolerated. This incident has been very difficult for this Board to handle because of Captain Kenny Taylor's past conduct. By the same token, there have been, of course, several allegations in the past of excessive force used by him." Griffin then turned to Lockhart and asked if any of the past allegations had been substantiated. Lockhart answered that they had not, either in court or disciplinary hearing. With that, Griffin entertained a motion for a disciplinary recommendation on Taylor. Dr. Wortham moved that the Board ask the Director to terminate Captain Taylor immediately with vacation pay. Elrod seconded the motion. When the vote was called for, Wortham and Elrod voted for the motion while Bevis and Dorsey opposed it. This meant that Griffin would have to vote to break the tie. Griffin voted "aye" and the motion to recommend termination for Taylor was passed.

After the vote, Bevis made a motion that Taylor be given the opportunity to resign as opposed to being terminated. The motion was seconded by Elrod and it passed unanimously.

The consideration of only one more employee remained, Captain A. G. Lucas. Griffin pointed out that Lucas was involved in several incidents but was not a primary player in any of them. According to La Plante's investigation, Lucas was involved in the altercations involving Ruiz, Norton, and Brown. In all the instances, La Plante stated that the complaints of the use of excessive force were sustained by clear and convincing evidence. It should be pointed out, however, that in all these altercations, Lucas was not the primary aggressor. He played a supporting role in each incident.

A motion was made by Elrod to find that Lucas had used excessive force. When Griffin called for a vote, only two board members voted in favor of the motion. Dorsey and Bevis did not vote. Griffin ruled that the motion passed. When challenged by

Elrod whether the motion passed, Griffin said that it did because a majority of those voting voted in the affirmative, but just to make sure, Griffin indicated that he voted "aye" which made three votes in the affirmative.

Next came the motion to recommend discipline. The motion by Dr. Wortham was to recommend Lucas be reduced one rank, from captain to lieutenant, placed on probation for six months, and be reminded that his job description only includes food service and that his activities be limited to food service only. It was seconded by Dorsey and was passed unanimously.

With these actions, the Board completed the task of recommending discipline for those who had been accused of using excessive physical force on January 1-2. After Board investigation, one was exonerated, one was terminated, and five received various levels of discipline. Nine employees were exonerated by never being called before the Board.

In the question-and-answer session with the media, Griffin made a couple of observations that added a little flesh to the Board's reasoning and actions. In his response to Victoria Hirschland of the *Pine Bluff Commercial* as to whether the Consent Decree was violated, Griffin said, "...parts of it were violated. We do not find that there is consistent violation or that it is habitual violation. We must remember that what has made this extremely difficult is that this matter was all brought about by the inmates in maximum security taking control of the maximum security building and taking six hostages and in … injuring one of the hostages. We feel like there was overreaction after a cooling off period had existed. In other words, we judged this in different time intervals. At the time the Department was taking control of the East Building and releasing the hostages, we realize that they must act with force, they must act with a positive and definite conduct. After control of the building was obtained and after the hostages were released, then there was less force needed, in our opinion, to maintain control of the East Building. And it was at this time, we feel excessive force existed, and we've just got to get our employees to realize that as the circumstances and conditions change, their conduct and their force must change."

At one point during the questioning, Griffin indicated that Taylor admitted that he used excessive force "in one of the incidents" (presumably in the Norton altercation). Griffin went on to say that if not for the Consent Decree, the punishment probably would not have been as severe, perhaps a 30-day suspension instead of termination, but the Board felt it was necessary to show the federal court that the Board was making a good faith effort to comply with the Consent Decree.

When Lockhart was pressed by Wayne Jordan of the *Arkansas Gazette* about whether Lockhart kicked Blaylock or not, Lockhart replied, "During the brief taking of that facility, then he (Blaylock) was brought to the front of the building and in an attempt to try to find out what was going on, where he came from where the other hostages were, if there were any more and if anybody was hurt, where and what extent, I told him to get up off the floor. I wanted to talk to him. He would not get up. He accused me of kicking, and I was standing there, as close as to Mr. Lyford. I did tell him to get up. He got up very reluctantly and would not cooperate in the interview. I did turn him around. He was facing the wall prior to me turning him around. I took him by the left shoulder with my right hand and jerked him around. I identified myself and asked him who he was and asked him questions about where the other employees were, if there were any more or where he came from, how many more inmates were involved in it, and he failed to cooperate with the interview. At that point, the interrogation was over with." Lockhart went on to say, "I did not step on his ankle. This was the last inmate that I talked to in the taking of the facility. I talked to him and then I immediately left the facility knowing that the facility was under control."

It was clear that the Board thought that the incidents in the La Plante report were not as severe as the report described. Wortham, a medical doctor, said that as he "read the Compliance report, I was horrified at the description of Barney Norton's injury. To read the description, I was expecting, as a physician, to come down here and see that man beat half to death. Okay, I see his picture and I go look at him, and as a physician, I recognize that he has not been beaten to death. He's been hit on the head. He's got three lacerations but has not gotten a brutal beating."

Near the end of the question-and-answer session, Bevis said, "I want to go on record as saying that I think Mr. La Plante, in some instances and in some cases, totally over-reacted on behalf of the inmate." To this, Griffin responded, "This is why we've moderated our findings of fact as compared to (La Plante's report). With that, the Board adjourned.

Within days after the board meetings, Director Mabry followed through on the discipline. Kenny Taylor was allowed to resign before any discipline was imposed and did so on April 10. The others received the discipline that was recommended to Mabry by the Board.

The Board, however, was not through with the employee matters. Two officers, Jesse Tillar and E. W. Smith, appealed the imposition of their discipline after Director Mabry had followed the Board's recommendation. The Board heard the appeals at their May 24 meeting, one in the morning session, and one in the afternoon. Both were held in executive session. In the morning, the Board heard from Jesse Tillar. Tillar had received six months' probation for refusing to take the polygraph test and demotion from lieutenant to sergeant for using excessive physical force. After reconvening from executive session, the Board voted to uphold six months' suspension, but reverse the decision to demote Tillar. By its vote, the Board was effectively exonerating Tillar from the charge of using excessive force. Although, as chairman, Griffin did not vote, he indicated later that he would have voted not to overturn Tillar's punishment.

In the afternoon session, the Board went into executive session to hear the appeal of E. W. Smith, who was represented by an attorney, Fred Davis. Smith had been placed on six months' probation for refusing to take the polygraph test and demoted from lieutenant to sergeant for using excessive force on Inmate Ruiz. After the executive session, the Board voted unanimously to "affirm the decision of the Director as to Sergeant Smith's case and deny his appeal."

Chapter 32

The Aftermath

After the April 7 Board meeting, it is not surprising that the attorney for the inmates, Philip Kaplan, was outraged with the Board's actions. In an article in the *Pine Bluff Commercial* on April 10, Kaplan indicated that he would file a motion in federal court asking that Judge Eisele read the compliance coordinator's report, find the officials not in compliance with the consent decree, and find the Board and Department in contempt of court. Kaplan went on to say that he felt the appropriate decision would have been to fire all the employees who were accused in the report of excessive physical force. Kaplan did in fact file such a motion, with the state attorney general's office filing a counter motion saying that the Corrections Board acted "responsibly, prudently, and completely on the report of the Compliance Coordinator, with a view solely toward complying with the terms of the Consent Decree." There was never a contempt of court issued by the judge. The matter, for the most part, was over.

There were, however, still several unresolved issues. The focus had been on the Department and the actions of the employees so much, that the inmates and their actions had largely gone unnoticed. An inmate had assaulted an officer. Several inmates had taken over the East Building and held several guards hostage. Ten inmates had scaled the fence and escaped. Eventually, however, charges were filed and the cases slowly worked their way through the judicial system.

CID Investigator Jack Ursery and Prosecuting Attorney Wayne Matthews continued working on these cases into the middle of 1980. The inmates were charged with battery, kidnap, and escape in Lincoln County, Arkansas. Five inmates (McKee, Pucilowski, Howell, Morse, and Blaylock) took a plea bargain deal, had the battery and kidnap charges dropped, and received four years for escape. Their new sentence was to run consecutively with their current sentences. When a sentence runs consecutively, the time is added to the time they are already serving. For example, if an inmate has a 20-year sentence and then gets a four-year sentence to run consecutively, the sentence will then become 24 years.

On August 14, 1980, Jerome Bargo pled guilty to an escape charge, after kidnap and battery charges had been dropped, and received a six-year sentence to run concurrently with his existing sentence. When a charge runs concurrently, it means that there is no additional time added to the current sentence. The concurrent sentence is served along with the existing sentence.

Johnny Wiggins, the inmate who assaulted Officer Bryant at the beginning of the takeover, negotiated a plea bargain deal and pled guilty to battery, kidnapping, and escape on October 31, 1979. He received five years for each charge for a total of 15 years. They were to run consecutively with his current sentence.

Three inmates held out for a jury trial. Paul Ruiz was tried in Lincoln County on June 24, 1981. He was found guilty of kidnapping and escape and received a total of 15 years to run consecutively with his current sentence. These added years didn't matter since Ruiz had a death sentence. He, along with Van Denton, was eventually executed on January 8, 1997.

Willie Brown and Ronnie Briggs had a jury trial on August 21, 1980, in Lincoln County. Brown's battery charge was dismissed by the judge before the trial began, and he was acquitted by the jury on the kidnapping and escape charges. Presumedly the jury took into account that Brown never actually left the East Building on January 1, only his cell. Briggs was found guilty of escape and was sentenced to one year to run consecutively with his current sentence.

Barney Norton, true to his nature, ended up beating the charges. He, along with his attorney, filed motion after motion, and used stall tactic after stall tactic, until finally three terms of court had passed without a trial. Norton then petitioned the Arkansas Supreme Court saying that he was denied a speedy trial. The Supreme Court ruled in Norton's favor on July 8, 1981; therefore he could not be tried on the charges.

Ismet Divanovich was not tried on his charges for a different reason. He had first been convicted of murder in November 1978, but the Arkansas Supreme Court overturned his conviction in November 1980. A new trial was ordered and in July 1981, after one mistrial, Divanovich was found innocent of the previous murder conviction, thus making the escape charges a moot point.

The January 1 event was not without some positive outcomes. At the March 30, 1979, board meeting, Director Mabry presented a curriculum for a four-week, pre-service training program for new employees. New recruits would learn about such subjects as personnel policies, rules and regulations, radio communication, history of the Department, as well as weapons training. The need for training surfaced during the investigation following the January 1 escape. Several officers spoke of meager or no training prior to being given the responsibility of supervising inmates.

The Board also recognized the need for an Internal Affairs Department within the ADC. Board Chairman Richard Earl Griffin talked extensively about this at the April 7, 1979, board meeting. He recommended that an investigative department be established, and that George Brewer head it. He made the following observation during the board meeting, "The reports that we received immediately after the January 1 and 2 incident, you can't characterize them maybe as being false, but you can certainly characterize them as being incomplete. They were not thorough." He further stated that sometimes the person who is doing the investigation may be the one who needs to be investigated. He went on to encourage Mr. Brewer not to get "entangled with the internal affairs of the different units and different divisions."

There were also some physical improvements made at Cummins that helped deter future escapes. Rolls of concertina wire were added to the top of the fence. Concertina wire is a type of barbed wire that is designed to snag clothing in such a way that makes it very difficult to get loose from the barbs. The barbs are also very sharp and can easily cut through flesh. In addition, a taller perimeter fence was built about 10 feet outside the current fence which meant inmates would have to scale two fences instead of one. These improvements vastly decreased the number of inmates who attempted to escape by scaling the perimeter fences.

After a rough and rugged road, the Arkansas Department of Corrections met the terms of the Consent Decree. Finney v. Mabry was dismissed by Judge G. Thomas Eisele on August 20, 1982, thus declaring the system constitutional. It had been a long journey since the first case, Holt v. Sarver, was filed in 1969 declaring certain practices of the prison unconstitutional. The Department matured during the 13 years it was under litigation. It had become less archaic and more in line with modern penological practices.

The January 1 incident has been described as a fulcrum or paradigm shift for the Department. It forced the Department to take a long look in the mirror and evaluate the common practices of the Department compared to what it should be doing. It was the perfect storm and like most storms, what came out on the other side was stronger and better.

The End

About the Author

William "Dubs" Byers, EdD, served 39 years with the Arkansas Corrections School System. He spent 20 years at Cummins as a teacher and principal in the school for inmates. In addition, he served 19 years in the central office as assistant superintendent and superintendent.

After his retirement in 2014, he served as pastor of First Baptist Church in Dumas, Arkansas, for five years. He currently serves on the Arkansas Board of Corrections, having been appointed by Governor Asa Hutchinson. Dubs has always had a keen interest in prison history and has an extensive collection of photos and memorabilia, along with hours of taped interviews with former employees and inmates.

Dubs grew up in Hope, Arkansas. He and his wife, Jane, have been residents of Gould, Arkansas, since 1975.

www.ingramcontent.com/pod-product-compliance
Lightning Source LLC
Chambersburg PA
CBHW050020100426
42739CB00011B/2723